GO Ahead!
Be Brave-ER

BENITA TYLER

ISBN: 978-0-9856964-9-8

First Edition 2021

Published in the United Stated by
Beloved Daffodils Inspirations - Kokomo, Indiana 46902

Dedications

This book is dedicated to my two daughters: Jasmine Allen and Cenia Tyler, my step-daughters: Tyeshia Clark, and Kandi Harvvard, along with my daughter-in-law: Emma Allen, and granddaughters: Zariyah, Miyarah, Journee, Correyah, Khali, and Luna, along with all my future unborn granddaughters. I'm grateful for my loving husband Cedric D. Tyler, my "Hype man", business partner, and best friend. He's my biggest fan. Special thanks to Jasmine Allen my daughter and project manager. A better version of me and helpmate. Your guidance is always needed and is never forgotten. I thank my mother Ann Benn for her example and strength as a single mother. Special thanks to my best friend Dewanna Dallas for unknowingly teaching me how to be braver in those early days of my life. A special shout out to some trailblazers in my community. These special women have embraced me and have been great examples of excellence: Dr. Christy Jenkins, Kristianna Upchurch, Tanika Forestal, Kalena James, Tanya Foutch, Danille Williams, Dee Thornton, Lori Minor, Sabrina Wilds, Liz Kerns, Katara McCarty, Stephanie Oden, Alicia Ramsey, and many more. Finally, I wouldn't be the woman I am today without the phenomenal women who have inspired me throughout the years: Dr. Joyce Myers, Lisa Nichols, Iyanla Vanzant, and Cheryl Wood, Oprah Winfrey, and Sarah Jakes. I consider these women to be part of my tribe. It has been their words and wisdom that resonates with me. They have the ability to penetrate my whole heart. They are #PHENOMENALWOMENONSTEROIDS.

Table of Contents

Foreword

GO Ahead! Be Brave-ER can be described as what I refer to as the anthem for all women. Can we agree that 2020 was a tough year where we experienced transformation in some areas and loss in others? However, there is a silver lining; a lot of women ROCKED 2020 by being triumphant in business. It's never too late to become Brave-ER in every area you were destine to be. Being brave-ER is something that I hope you will not only adopt but implement. Don't forget to share this powerful mantra with other women and girls who are close to you. The earlier we grab ahold of this mission to be brave-ER, the better chance we'll have at executing our ability to handle any situation life throws at us. We've made lemonade out of lemons, but there's still work to do. It's never too late to adopt a positive mindset or to learn life lessons from those willing to share. It's called growth. I encourage women to be brave, but do not to stop there; take things a step farther by being Brave-ER. It's brave to the 100th power. YOU'RE capable of doing great and necessary work. The dictionary defines the word 'BE' as a verb that is used to talk about a feeling or state. I give you permission to go forth and 'BE' (Having a Confident State of Mind) Brave-ER, (ready to face and endure challenges in life and showing up with courage) Let's take this journey together. I can't wait to see how brave you will become.

"For what it's worth:
It's never to late, or, in my case,
too early, to be whoever you want to be.
There's no time limit.
Stop whenever you want.
You can change or stay the same.
There are no rules to this thing.
W can make the best of the worst of it.
I hope you see things that startle you.
I hope you feel things you've never felt before.
I hope you meet people
with a different point of view.
I hope you live a life you are proud of.
If you find that you are not,
I hope you have the courage
to start all over again."

– F. Scott Fitzgerald

Chapter 1

Brave-ER - Self-Esteem

Y‌ou've heard of the big bad bogeyman, right? He's that legendary baddie who scares you shitless and then takes up residence in the back of your mind while waiting patiently to expose the skeletons hidden in the depths. Once he gets a grip, he'll pull out his script and begin taunting you. He strategically tortures you with a combination of past failures and recent regrets. We detest him for being so damn good at his job. His actions could win him an Academy Award. You better take cover, because when he decides to strike, he'll leave you feeling afraid and unable to move. You won't have the strength or desire to get through the next chapter of life. It's not only you that he picks on. No one is safe; he enjoys taunting everyone. However, he gets the most bang for his buck by targeting women and he reports that we're the easiest. It doesn't take much for him to shake our confidence until it's lost and we become paralyzed in his grip.

That's right, he comes to steal, kill, and destroy everything important to us. We make things too easy for him, and we trust him blindly as he disguises himself as those who we love or the people unworthy of our time and attention. All of a sudden, our dreams vanish just like that and we spend our entire lifetime vexed while trying to get rid of him for good. We can't allow him to win. It's time to put on your big-girl panties and become brave-ER in the fight.

It's not surprising to find the bogeyman sitting on your shoulders when you awake from a restless night of sleep. You head to the bathroom sink to start your day. The culprit blocks the mirror and you push him out of the way. He's aware that it's in the morning time when you are feeling the most self-conscious. Right in the middle of washing your face and brushing your teeth in your tattered pajamas, he glares at you. He tries to get a reaction by reminding you that those tattered pajamas you refuse to throw away aren't enough to protect you. They no longer serve as a safety blanket. You realize that he's telling the truth, when all of a sudden you hear him using your thoughts against you: "You're not pretty enough," or, "Look! There's another pimple on your nose," or, "You're so ugly," and, "Your hips are wider than they were yesterday."

He becomes larger than life as he rips off the band-aid barely sticking to your skin. He exposes the guilt and shame you feel but are not ready to deal with. He taunts you by playing a continuous loop of his taunts in your head, and you feel like you're going crazy.

"Are you going to fight back?" I implore you to go ahead and be brave-ER. Don't fall for his lies. The truth is: You are in control of your thoughts, words, and actions, and you get to choose the life you want to live. It's all up to you. Tell the bogeyman that he's not all that scary. Take a deep breath and warn him in your sternest voice to flee, "You are no longer my judge, jury, or executioner."

The bogeyman realizes that fear is a factor and explains why it is so easy for him to rattle us. Fear allows him to have his way because we've lost the will to fight after putting up with his antics for years. However, we're not helpless, and we have to decide to take action with a sense of urgency. One way to do so is to seek the assistance of a trusted friend or family member who has not only faced the bogeyman but has defeated him.

> *Keep in mind that when trusted friends answer the call to provide advice, you should be open to receiving it.*

Keep in mind that when trusted friends answer the call to provide advice, you should be open to receiving it. Don't allow your foolish pride to get in the way by believing that their advice can't be applied to your situation. Yet again, this is the bogeyman manipulating you. He doesn't want you to break free of him. Just think: Some of the advice given is worth applying, but you have to be brave enough to believe that it can be helpful. Go ahead; build up your stamina. You're going to need it if you expect to defeat the bogeyman whose chasing after you. He has a lot more experience than you do, and without making an effort to get rid of him, once and for all, he will continue to rear his ugly head in every situation.

Have you ever met a woman who seems to have lost her self-worth? Her survival seems to be rooted in keeping up with the Joneses or trying to be something that she's not. Her behavior can be tied to the "Imposter syndrome". That is where she feels like a fraud even though she realizes that not living an authentic life is serving her well. I believe that we've all been there at some point in our lives. However, together we can debunk the behavior that causes us to try and be someone who God never intended.

Repeat after me, "I am a competent, capable, and intelligent woman who can do anything I put my mind to."

That feels empowering, right? We have to choose to live an authentic life that reflects our unique beauty and promise. Show the world your greatness. Other women are waiting to learn from you. The alternative is to be an imposter who allows the bogeyman to seize every moment while feeling like a failure. The latter choice allows for being in an anxious and depressed state. Ladies, we ain't got time for that. We have to feed our faith and our own belief in ourselves. Rise! "Do you have faith the size of a mustard seed?" We need faith to prevail, as it helps us to gain a renewed sense of pride and self-awareness. We simply can't afford to lose our faith. Far too many women have abandoned their dreams and have decided to live a life without joy and happiness. "Are you one of them?" The fact that you're reading this book means you very well could be. No worries! Let's work on this challenge together. We can build up our self-efficacy, which is defined as a person's belief in his or her ability to succeed in a particular situation. I don't know about you, but for me it sounds like the right attitude to have about ourselves. If we don't believe in ourselves, it will be difficult for everyone else to see our value.

I'm the first to admit that there have been times in my life when I have gotten off track. I've become so frustrated that I've thrown up my arms in defeat and counted myself out. It's funny how we are the ones who count ourselves out the most. Those are the times I refer to as "Dark times". However, with healed scars as evidence of my victory, I'd like to offer you some strategies that helped me. Pushing up against the wall I've felt like a caged bird. That is until I decided to fight the bogeyman with prayer knowing full well that prayer is the one thing that could hold him off from hurting me any longer. My first action step was to ask God to release me from the stronghold the bogeyman had on me. I was too weak to fight back and my strength was depleted. I knew that I needed to be brave-ER and to be able to trust myself to keep praying faithfully to win.

Our sovereign God reminded me that He had already equipped me with the tools necessary to defeat the bogeyman. I needed to use them. He pressed upon me the urgency to do my part and revealed the consequences of continuing to be afraid. Asking God to slay the bogeyman for me were the pleas of a coward and rooted in fear. If God did all the work for me, I wouldn't experience the growth and maturity needed to reach my full potential. With the faith that God was on my side, I began to pray and fight the bogeyman. Brave moments ebbed and flowed as I fought.

I admit that most moments they ebbed until my confidence increased. I began to look for help from others too, but God reminded me to be cautious. It's not a good idea to let everyone in your life in on your trials and tribulations. It's important to develop self-awareness, because it helps us to discern what we need and who is meant to help us. It's time for you to come to terms with the things that make you afraid. God has equipped you with what you need to win.

It took me years to develop the habit of doing the work necessary to achieve the positive changes that I desired in my life. When God realized that I was serious, He partnered with me by providing better strategies than the ones I could think of on my own. I felt like more than a conquer. His voice was clear and astounding when He said to me, *"Benita, go forth and be brave-ER."*

I accepted His words as my truth and took action. At that moment, my eyes welled up and tears began to roll down my face. I knew that He wouldn't steer me wrong. I realized that I hadn't been able to rely on my earthly father during times of despair and marveled at the fact that God's love is superior to any love that an earthly father can provide. He loves us and showers us with His perfect love. His parenting style is the perfect blend of correction and love. Embrace it and be brave-ER just like me.

God's grace has shown up during many periods in my life. He's covered me as I've stood on mountains to celebrate wins, leaving no stones unturned. Equally, He's been with me those times when I've fallen into the darkest pits in the valley of darkness, and God pulled me out. I recall cowering in the face of fear and hiding to avoid facing my worst critics. I've swallowed my pride to ask for help from others even though doing so is not one of my strengths. I can report that I'm getting better at it. In the past, asking for help has caused me unnecessary grief because I looked in the wrong places for assistance. I've concluded that there is nothing wrong with asking for help from your spouse or a trusted friend. Two brains are better than one and they are able to help me brainstorm to come up with a workable plan. Asking for help allows me to be brave-ER while on the journey.

Have you laid down in your bed at night only to have your mind wander as you entertained thoughts that were so heavy that you could not have fallen asleep? Or, have you cried into your pillow to avoid your significant other hearing you because you don't want to admit that you're having a hard time, only to awaken to a beautiful sunny morning that's filled with hope and possibilities? You praise God, knowing that He confirms that He's pleased with you. God loves to celebrate moments when we're stronger and more brave-ER than we were yesterday. The beauty is that we are provided with 1,440 minutes every day to make a better choice in areas of need and be proactive.

Having the bogeyman take up residence in your head means you are responsible for taming him. Even in your strength, he's lurking around waiting for the perfect moment to reveal your darkest secrets. I remember the moment he ruined my life by telling me a lie so big that it would take a lifetime to debunk. It was a body-shaming lie that penetrated my soul, leaving an indelible imprint. I was an impressionable ten years old, with a lot of life ahead of me and new things to learn about myself. Why wouldn't I believe him? There wasn't a person in my immediate circle feeding me anything to contradict the lie he told. The bogeyman is cruel and will use any means to make you feel insecure.

He got right in my face to yell the big lie, "Benita, you've got a big butt! Look at it sitting there on your back like a basketball," he asserted.

That's all it took for me to believe something was wrong with me. Like most girls, I was attempting to come into my own while trying to accept my God-given traits. It doesn't take a lot to ruin our self-esteem. When we hear something negative, we start to question if our bodies are normal and if we are good enough. I hated the fact that the bogeyman gave me something to worry about so early in my life. It was difficult to find the answers I was seeking. I didn't think I fit into society. The bogeyman was causing me pain while laughing in my face. We allow the bogeyman to go unchecked because we are afraid of him.

He wins! My mind was filled with negative body-shaming thoughts. If that wasn't bad enough, he enlisted the help of my friends and family. How rude!

They quickly followed his lead and believed that teasing me was fun. They didn't consider the implications with their clever little slogans, such as, "Benita-Benn-Bear with her big booty and her Bear and her Bottle, and her . . ." Well, you get the message.

Needless to say, their fun was detrimental to my self-esteem. During those years, I already felt awkward about my height. I was taller than most ten-year-old girls. Every time I looked in the mirror, I saw a pair of skinny legs that held up my butt. My legs looked like two pencils at the bottom. I didn't have any issues with my upper body. The bogeyman used my butt to mess me up. I didn't want anyone to look at it. It wasn't until I was in my twenties that I realized big butts were the in-thing. There wasn't anything wrong with my butt. When the butt craze hit in the late 2000s, it confirmed that big butts were in high demand and that women were willing to pay thousands for them even if it meant dying on the operating table.

The bigger and rounder, the better, is what men think about butts. Just ask Sir-Mix-A-Lot, when in 1992 he made a song called "Baby Got Back" that permitted curvy women to flaunt their big butts. It was a huge success. God blessed me with a normal butt. He does works in mysterious ways. However, not withstanding being bullied and teased, it is difficult for young girls to carry the weight of being tormented about how they look. Girls believe every word spoken about their bodies — literally.

To cope, I started hiding myself and my body parts from others. I wore sweaters and coats even on the hottest of days. They served as comfort blankets and were a way to distract others from giving me unwanted attention. My self-esteem was depleted day by day, but fortunately for me, I was eventually able to fill my cup with positivity and laughter when out with friends. We rise as my brave meter rise went up and all of a sudden, I found myself able to rid of my mind of the negative thoughts about my body whenever they popped up in my head.

Once I made it to high school, I was tested. Would I be able to break free from the complex I had about my butt? Everyone knows that high school boys are mannish and have raging hormones. They get their thrills by making girls feel self-conscious. The boys at my high school were no different. I indeed gave them plenty to look at. I was an attractive 5'6" and 125 lbs with a bright smile. In fact, I officially earned the distinction of "Best smile" my senior year. The senior boys had their sights on the in-coming sophomore girls to flirt with. I happened to be one of those girls who received a lot of attention from them. Some of the attention was welcomed and some wasn't. A lot of those senior boys were good-looking. Their girlfriends made me feel uncomfortable whenever they gave me dirty looks. They saw me as a threat after learning that I was on the "Fine Sophomore List". I didn't ask for the attention, and feeling like an object on display wasn't my choice either.

I felt awkward in the presence of a group of boys. I despised having close contact with them... like while slow dancing. I wanted no part of it. My sister, who is two years older than me, liked the attention. She would drag me to parties, and her friends would try to teach me how to slow dance in one of our neighbor's garage. When we walked into the parties, two or three of the boys would ask that dreaded question when a slow jam was playing, "Would you like to dance?"

Yikes! was the response going off in my head. I'd turn them down in an instant while trying to find a place in the darkness to wait for my sister to be ready to go home.

We lived a few miles from my high school. It wasn't unusual during the late '70s for kids to walk miles to and from school with friends. It was a lot of fun. The air was filled with laughter and no one had a care in the world. Sometimes a fight would break out making it less fun. Lincoln High School was a predominately Black high school that was notorious for its athletic programs. Our homecomings were over-the-top. The alumni were eager to come back to celebrate. Our athletes excelled in sports such as basketball, football, and track, and it was a blast to watch them. Some of those athletes were the boys who congregate on the corners leading to the school's front entrance. They flirted with any girl who walked past them. I'd try my best to avoid them at all costs, even if it meant not making eye contact with any of them. It didn't work; they flirted anyway.

During the 10th grade, I kept to myself while participating in what I like to describe as nerdy activities, one of which was a club called the Hornet Hustlers. The club's goal was to make those large paper banners that our football players busted through either at the beginning of the game or at the end of halftime. One of the perks of belonging to the Hornet Hustlers was that we got into our football games free. I loved sitting in the stands and got hyped in the cheer block section of the stands.

We had the best jazz band. They played all of the latest songs while swaying back and forth. They helped the crowd get their groove on. It was always a blast. I also loved to watch the cheerleaders from afar. I repeated their cheers and chants and clapped when prompted. If you ask me, I was the ultimate fan who had a lot of school spirit.

I had previous experience with being the ultimate fan. When I was in the eighth grade, I went to live with my best friend and her family. I lived there for about a year and a half. Her family adopted me as a cousin, and being that I didn't have a lot of family members, I was happy to be their cousin. After graduating from the eighth grade, we enrolled at Mt. Miguel High School whose school body consisted of 9th - 12th graders.

> *I hadn't considered trying out for cheerleader at Lincoln but that old bogeyman reminded me that if I started thinking that way I'd be wasting my time.*

My cousin and I became popular quickly and were part of the handful of minorities who attended the school. We decided to try out for freshman cheerleaders together. Unfortunately, I didn't make the squad but my cousin did. I was happy for her. I was one of her biggest fans, cousin, and personal hairstylist. I attended all of her cheer practices and games. I cheered in the stands, and it was an awesome experience. I hadn't considered trying out for cheerleader at Lincoln but that old bogeyman reminded me that if I started thinking that way I'd be wasting my time. He asserted that I wouldn't make it even if I tried.

"Oh, Benita, been there done that. It won't work this time either," the bogeyman forcefully contended.

I accepted his words as the truth. I believed that the odds were stacked against me since every activity or sport was competitive. Being a cheerleader at Lincoln High was a bigger deal than it was at Mt. Miguel. The cheerleaders were like sorority sisters. They shared a close-knit sisterhood, and after graduating, they came back to Homecoming every year. It was impressive to see some of them who had been out of school for ten years. Surprisingly, most of them could still fit into their uniforms. They made the memories magical, especially when our football players won the game. School spirit exploded like fireworks on the 4th of July.

The summer before my junior year, I received an offer that would prove to be life changing. I love watching people. I would go as far as saying that it's a habit. I recall sitting on the school lawn one summer afternoon enjoying my surroundings as the sun shined down on my face. I felt happy to be in that place at that time to watch the junior and senior varsity football players practicing. Little League was big in our community as well, so the little leaguers usually practiced during the same times making the football field an assortment of exciting activities for me to enjoy watching.

The cheerleaders were also on the field practicing for the upcoming tryouts. I entertained the thought of what it would be like to be in their shoes as I sat on the grass still wearing my coat even though it was hot as hell. I stayed out of the way and unnoticed, well... that is until an old acquaintance who was practicing for cheerleader began walking over in my direction.

"Hey, Benita, we're practicing for the JV tryouts. Do you want to try out with us?" she asked.

At first I gave her a blank stare as I tried to wrap my mind around what she was offering me. She wasn't bothered by my lack of engagement. She kept talking, "Do you remember me? I'm Dee. We met a long time ago. I met you and your sister at the park," she reminded me.

"I do remember you," I responded.

I was frozen at that moment and wondered if her proposal was worth taking. There were a couple of things in play that I needed to consider. The first was the fact that the JV Cheer Squad would consist of 10th graders and I was in the 11th grade and should've been trying out for the Varsity Squad. The second was that I didn't want to feel rejected if I didn't make it, or worse, ridiculed by others. I worried about what everyone would think if I cheered for the JV. A flood of emotions consumed me, but I pushed past them. I didn't allow the bogeyman to win this time.

All of a sudden, I jumped up to my feet, tore off the coat that served me as a security blanket, and hurried across the field with Dee to learn the practice cheer. All of my self-conscious thoughts about my butt were frozen in time, and I was happy for the opportunity to be brave-ER in becoming a cheerleader. I stood out there on the lawn that day with my insecurities exposed before my peers to do something that I had always wanted to do. I studied every movement that was being taught to me. My confidence began to shoot through the roof once I realized that the practice cheer was easy for me to learn.

Then, out of nowhere, the bogeyman visited me. He began torturing me and reminding me that I couldn't do a proper cartwheel and that my athletic abilities were next to zero when it came to flipping or anything related to gymnastics. I put the execution of a cartwheel right up there with swimming. Both of these activities were things that made me afraid. I propagated the lie told to me by the bogeyman and believed that I wasn't brave enough to trust my feet to leave the ground while attempting to execute a cartwheel and that swimming wasn't safe for me either. The bogeyman was basing his lies on my past experiences, and so far, he was successful.

My cousin's parents had an in-the-ground pool in their backyard. They loved to swim and were good at it. My younger cousins loved to do flips and tricks in the deep end that reminded me that my role at the pool was to dig and kick my feet in the water while sitting in the shallow end. I knew my boundaries and was willing to keep them.

One summer Saturday evening, her parents had a party in the backyard. I remember everyone congregated around the pool near the deep end to watch my cousins show off their impressive tricks while jumping off the diving board. I decided to join in by sitting closer to the deep end to watch. I hadn't respected the boundaries that I made for myself. My mother had been invited to the party and brought a date. Everyone was having a great time before my mother's date decided to play a practical joke on me. He assumed that I could swim since I was wearing a bathing suit and sitting poolside. He snuck up in back of me and threw me into the deep end. I quickly sank to the bottom of their 12-foot-deep pool. I went in a panic state not knowing how to swim. As I went deeper into the water, my first instincts were to kick my feet and flail my arms like I had seen my cousins do for years, but the water rushed into my mouth. I felt out of control, as I believed that I was going to choke to death as the water clogged my orifices. A few bystanders jumped into the pool to save me. They got me out of the water and onto the concrete as they patted me on my back and encourage me to spit the water out that was causing me to choke. I recall being so embarrassed. I ran into the house to escape the crowd, still upset. I cried hysterically as my cousin comforted me.

"Are you okay?" she asked.

"I can't go back out there," I told her nervously.

"He didn't know you couldn't swim. Will you be okay in here by yourself?" she asked.

I appreciated my cousin's concern, and as I look back on that experience, I wonder why the adults responsible for me hadn't come inside to check on me. My cousin said that she understood how I felt and that I didn't want to go back outside.

I told her, "You should go back out there and enjoy yourself. I'll be okay."

She agreed to come in to check on me throughout the night. My mother came in to check on me. She was furious with her date and had given him a good telling-off right out there in front of everybody.

"Benita, Earl said he's so sorry. He didn't know that you couldn't swim," she reported.

"I know! I should not have sat there; it's not his fault," I spoke.

I accepted his apology because it wasn't his fault. He was doing what most pranksters do at pool parties when people sit by the deep end. He didn't know a lot about me and the fact that I couldn't swim. The fact that I almost drowned did nothing to make me feel brave-ER when it comes to swimming that day. I still can't swim and have no desire to learn, but I do love to soak up the sun either poolside or at the beach. Learning to swim remains an area of growth for me.

At cheer tryouts, when the judges called my number, I felt anxious as I walked onto the stage in our auditorium to try out for the JV Cheer Squad. I stood on the spot marked on the floor with tape. I took a deep breath, smiled, and said, "Ready-Okay," before performing the required cheer. I surprised myself by doing a much better cartwheel than I expected and I performed the cheer perfectly. My decision to remain positive and to be brave-ER paid off that time. When the results were posted for who made the JV Squad, I was thrilled that my name was on the list. Finally I had become a cheerleader, and to top it off, I was later voted captain of the squad. Every time I put on my cheer uniform, I felt a little more brave-ER. Cheerleading was the activity that increased my confidence. It allowed me to morph into an unstoppable version of myself. Benita believed she was the bomb. My popularity grew that next year, and by the time tryouts rolled around for the Varsity Cheer Squad the following year, I was brave enough to try out without being nudged. I made the Varsity Cheer Squad with ease, making my years at Lincoln High School some of the best times of my life.

BE Brave-ER

What has feeling unstoppable looked like for you?

Is there a time you experienced a feeling worth duplicating in your life?

What lessons in your life do you need to re-learn?

Can you recall a time when you forgot about what you were afraid of because you got a second chance at it?

What dreams have you allowed to be stolen?

What actions will you taking to turn your dreams into a reality?

What's stopping you from conquering your bogeyman?

What role have you played in holding yourself back from following your dreams?

What are some specific things can you do to become more self-aware?

Chapter 2

Brave-ER - Motherhood

Being a woman of faith causes me to have an awareness of the importance of having a personal relationship with God. He and I have enjoyed many engaging and meaningful conversations over the years about my maternal instincts and my desire to embrace motherhood someday. I've allowed others to take advantage of me and waiting until I'm fed up with something or someone to call on God for help. Then I'd go to the extreme of unloading all of my mess on Him prior to thanking Him for His grace and mercy that He gives me freely. He has done many great things for me, including making me the mother of many and giving me twins. I'm grateful.

Sometimes women relinquish power to those unworthy, but I'm here to remind you that God is worthy, trusting, and a helpmate. It's better to rely on faith then it is to put your trust in failed people who may or may not have your back. We reap what we sow when we don't have God and positive people in our corner who can provide spiritual insight as needed. Those people encourage us to stay in the fight and to take their petitions to God in prayer. He will never leave or forsake us. These tips are the only way to take the reins of control back into our lives. While on the journey of motherhood, it's essential to build a circle of trusted women because they understand our plight and choices for motherhood. They are able to provide us with some insight on what works best while raising kids which I'm sure you'll agree is beneficial.

I encourage you to start this process today. Ask God to cover you and your family in all things every day. If you're not a believer in God, don't feel dismayed. Throughout this book, I'm happy to share my faith with you as a token of encouragement. Identify a spiritual mentor who's willing to speak positivity into your spirit. Remember,

> *Ask God to cover you and your family in all things every day.*

you are in charge of yourself and responsible for yourself. The person you worship is a private matter, but please be intentional about tapping into a spiritual source. You don't have to feel alone.

I was baptized when I was around eleven years old. A friend of my mother and a believer of God offered to take my sister and I to church. I'm not sure why my mother didn't go with us, but I'm glad she allowed us to attend church with her good friend. We attended occasionally and looked forward to going. The church was one of those Baptist churches with a large traditional choir. The members belted out Gospel lyrics with vigor and caused me to fall in love with Gospel Music. It's my serenity. I would sit quietly in the church house while observing the distinctive men and women who seemed to hang on to the preacher's every word. We liked going to church because we would have a few minutes to walk across the street to the store. We'd spend the money intended to put into the straw basket for the offering. I'm not sure if we had permission to go to the store, but like the other kids, we went anyway. While inside the sanctuary, I would marvel at how the congregation seemed to believe the words that the preacher read out of the Bible.

I also loved the church building; it was painted a beautiful tone of pink. The church could be seen as you drove down one of the main interstates. We went to the church for what seemed like a few summers and attended church camp. I loved making the crafts they taught us how to make.

It was a long time after that before I would walk into the House of the Lord. I wasn't having an active daily dialogue with God. The bogeyman was running rampant in my life. The more I believed that I could make choices about parenting and life in my strength, the more he attacked me. However, the good news is that I re-engaged in my relationship with God around 1998 after enrolling at Indiana Wesleyan University. I credit the university for its Christian teaching and inclusion. I began to yearn to be in God's presence again.

Allow me to take you along for the ride as I describe my encounters with motherhood. After graduating high school, I would describe myself as a young and confident woman who was full of purpose and believed that I had it all together. I attended San Diego State University in the fall of 1979 while working part-time at the San Diego Zoo. Life was carefree and I was enjoying a meaningful relationship with my best friend Dee. We had lots in common from our cheerleading days when we were inseparable. We enjoyed each other's company. We were living our lives out loud. Dee was the epitome of a fashionista and always looked sharp. She was unanimously voted 'Best Dressed' her senior year. Dee loved the arts, culture, and dance. Her father was an established actor who lived in Los Angeles. It's likely she inherited her vibrant personality and appreciation of the arts from him.

It wasn't too long before Dee's sense of fashion rubbed off on me. Our love for fashion intensified when we began working after high school. We paid good money for the latest fashions and shopped at trendy retail stores. We accessorized our outfits completely with earrings and cute shoes. Our outfits closely matched, but I wouldn't refer to us as the Bobbsey Twins. We added our signature look to our outfits to show off our individuality. We received a lot of compliments everywhere we went and earned the label "The sharp girls". We'd show up looking great at concerts, plays, and parties.

We loved to dance and didn't allow our great sense of fashion to stop us from getting sweaty on the dance floor. Dee was the better dancer. She could draw a crowd. They cheered her on loudly whenever she partnered with a high school friend of ours named Glen. They were fun to watch and were usually paired up to dance in the final contest of the night where they occasionally won the best dancer award.

Our friendship was rooted in love. I supported Dee in everything. While in high school she played softball for the school's team. I loved going to her games whenever her coach allowed me to ride the school bus with the team. Dee was good at Modern and African Dance. I always thought she'd become a famous actor like her father. Dee became a successful entrepreneur and influencer with a few successful businesses. I learned a lot of things from Dee. Unknowingly, Dee taught me how to be brave-ER and to try different things. I was along for the great ride and transformation.

Dee and I did a brave thing when we were nineteen. We decided to book a trip to Hawaii. We saved the money to pay for the trip. I loved the fact that we didn't play the victim or sit around sulking about the fact that we were raised by single mothers. We made lemonade out of lemons and kept things moving. While in Hawaii, we laid on the beach and sipped on virgin cocktails. We had a blast! I'll always remember that trip.

> *I put all of my energy into my boyfriend.*
> *I was jeopardizing my ability to enjoy connections and friendships with women.*

It wasn't too long after we returned from Hawaii that our friendship would be tested. It was time to make room for boyfriends. We decided to do so for different reasons. The enjoyment of our time together was beginning to dwindle. There was an obvious shift in me once I put all of my energy into my boyfriend. I was jeopardizing my ability to enjoy connections and friendships with women. Dee would be the last best friend that I would have going forward. Over the last forty years, I have yet to establish a close friendship like the one Dee and I enjoyed. Once I married, I would be focused on motherhood and being a wife. My life choices didn't belong to me, and little by little I handed over my power to my boyfriend.

When I was nineteen, I found out that I was pregnant. Being a mother meant I would experience happiness and I was ready to embrace it. Because of my love for kids, I didn't need to do anything to make myself a good mom. I was willing to choose motherhood at all costs even if it meant raising my child alone. I was prepared to be brave-ER in motherhood. It didn't seem like a scary proposition to be a single parent because my mother was actively modeling the art of single parenting to my sister and myself. She made things look easy while never complaining about her plight.

My boyfriend's family dynamics were different than mine, and I understood that he wasn't prepared to entertain the thought of an unplanned pregnancy. His immediate family represented the one I desired for myself. From the outside looking in, they seemed close. He was the youngest of six kids. He loved and respected his parents. He complied with their wishes and they believed that he could do nothing wrong. I realized that the fact that he was a college student didn't lend itself to becoming an unexpected father. It would be difficult for him to be brave-ER by telling his parents a baby was on the way. I hoped that he would respond with great joy, but he didn't. I pictured him responding like men on television who received similar news.

> *My mother was actively modeling the art of single parenting to my sister and myself. She made things look easy while never complaining about her plight.*

"I'm pregnant," I told him.

My boyfriend was numb. He didn't provide a verbal response. Instead, he went into fight or flight mode as he jumped out of the driver's seat of his car. He paced back and forth for what seemed like minutes. I realized at that moment that I gave him more news than he could handle.

"What do you plan to do?" he asked.

I hated his insensitive question. I didn't respond right away. Although he never came right out and asked me to have an abortion, it was obvious that it was the outcome he wanted. He looked scared. I decided to take the matter into my own hands, and it was me who made the difficult choice. I was distraught and the decision hurt me more than I was willing to communicate or advocate for myself. Neither of us was handling the situation like the young adults we were. We didn't involve our parents. I had considered my boyfriend's feelings over mine. I was empathic about how difficult it would be for him to find the courage to tell his parents. I forfeited my dreams of motherhood instead. The bogeyman cheered me on by convincing me that my boyfriend's situation trumped mine and the life growing inside of me wasn't anything important to consider. The bogeyman will force us to do things we're not comfortable with when we allow him to. He has no problem being a dream killer.

I wished my boyfriend had accepted his responsibility like most twenty-year-old young men do when faced with the same set of circumstances. Needless to say, I went ahead and called the abortion clinic to inquire about the costs. With the information in hand, I scheduled the appointment and told my boyfriend the date and time of the procedure. I hoped he would've responded by asked me to have his child, but nothing changed.

"Are you okay? I can take you," he offered.

"I will need you to drive me there," I told him.

I felt betrayed even though I was the one who was giving up my right to choose. There weren't any written rules that said I didn't need his permission to become a mom. I began to resent him and avoided his calls. On the dreaded day, my boyfriend drove me to the clinic. I was angry at myself for not asking him to pay at least half for the procedure. He never offered and that made me madder. It was my strong sense of independence that kicked in. I had gotten in my way, lost my voice, and done the opposite thing I wanted to do. It was on me,

I told myself, and I needed to resolve the situation quickly. I wished I had been brave-ER during that time. I should've told him that having my baby wasn't negotiable.

There is a danger in taking on more than you should in certain situations. You have to use your words to honor yourself. Failing to do so is not what being brave-ER means. When we arrived at the clinic, we were instructed to sit and wait in the lobby. I nervously waited for my name to be called.

"Benita," the woman sitting at the front desk called.

As I walked up to the doors leading to the back, I recall feeling like it was the worst day of my life. I'm not sure what thoughts were going through my boyfriend's head while he waited in the lobby. My thoughts were all over the place. I felt scared, guilty, helpless, and alone. After the procedure was over, I was taken to the recovery room where the other women who came there had made the same dreadful decision as me. After I came out from under the anesthesia, it felt like I was waking up after a terrible nightmare. I was hysterical. The attending nurse was heavy-handed with me in her response.

She asked me to calm down, "You need to calm down. You're upsetting the others," she spoke rudely.

I followed her instructions as I continued to mourn my loss. I was put off by her insensitivity. I regretted my actions, but it was too late. After about an hour, the nurse advised me that it was time for me to go home. I wanted to run out of the clinic without being seen but walked slowly to the lobby to meet my boyfriend. He stood up when I walked through the door and asked me if I was okay. However, the next few words that came out of his mouth were a "WTF" moment. I couldn't believe what I was hearing and wanted to punch him in the face.

"I wanted to come back there to get you," he said.

I couldn't allow any sound to come out of my mouth. I think I was in shock from his comment. I became furious with him. How could he come up with this epiphany so late in the game? I wondered why he couldn't brave-ER much earlier. We rode to my house in silence. I blamed myself for not putting my wants and needs ahead of his. I was willing to be supportive as he cowered to avoid upsetting his parents. We failed the child that God had blessed us with.

> *I blamed myself for not putting my wants and needs ahead of his.*

God gave me a 2nd chance to be brave-ER in my quest for motherhood. After being married to my first husband for a few years, I believed motherhood was on the horizon for me. We were enjoying an exciting dating life. We enjoyed the simple life, and our dates included things like going to 7/11 which was around the corner from our apartment. We'd play the game, Ms. Pac Man, for hours, and things would be competitive at times. Afterward, we go back to our apartment to share a pint of vanilla Haagen Dazs ice cream. We were married a couple of years before I shared that I wanted to start a family. However, my husband said he wasn't ready. I decided to go with the flow, hoping that he would quickly change his mind.

One day while cleaning my bedroom, I notice a box on the shelf in my closet. Inside was a copy of my husband's Holy Quran. I had been curious about it and decided to open it. I was intrigued. I wanted to learn more about his religious views and how they differed from mine. I found a beautiful photo of a baby boy right in the middle of the Quran. The baby boy was wearing a blue velvet one-piece outfit. I wondered who the baby belonged to and why my husband had the keepsake. I confronted him later that evening. To my surprise, I was chastised for roaming through his belongings. I was at a loss for words and couldn't understand why my question made him angry. After he had time to calm down, he admitted to me that the baby was his. He said that he and an old girlfriend back home had the baby together. The revelation of the baby made me feel betrayed. I didn't understand why he had hidden something so important from me. He attempted to justify his actions.

"I didn't think you would understand. You are so special to me. I thought you wouldn't accept a man who already had a child. Can you forgive me?" he asked.

He was right! A baby might have been a non-starter for me. I was a little judgmental back then. However, I couldn't get over the fact that he hadn't been honest. His child's existence affected us both. When I considered his answer for not wanting kids yet, I

I am forever thankful for the opportunity to experience motherhood.

believed that it wasn't fair for him to think he would dictate my choice to be a mother when he was already a father. The fact that we were already married was reason enough to have kids.

God agreed, as it wasn't too long before I learned that I was pregnant. When I told my husband, the bogeyman cheered. It was like déjà vu. My husband's response wasn't positive. He shut down and repeated that he didn't want any more kids. This time around, the choice was mine. It wasn't until I was in my second trimester that my husband embraced the idea. We gave birth to a healthy baby boy. I felt lucky to be my baby's mother. I embrace motherhood bravely. I couldn't take my eyes off my baby. He was perfect. I was happy with myself for standing my ground. The inception of life is a blessing and nothing can be taken for granted. Some women can't conceive. God has forgiven me and I forgave myself. He has trusted me to bring additional lives into the world. I am forever thankful for the opportunity to experience motherhood.

BE Brave-ER

How excited were you to embrace motherhood?

When experiencing a loss of pregnancy by choice or miscarriage, did you feel brave-ER to tell your story to other women to help them heal?

Have you forgiven yourself for making difficult decisions regarding motherhood?

When experiencing sadness resulting from conflicting parenting decisions, what are some ways to effectively communicate to get your point across?

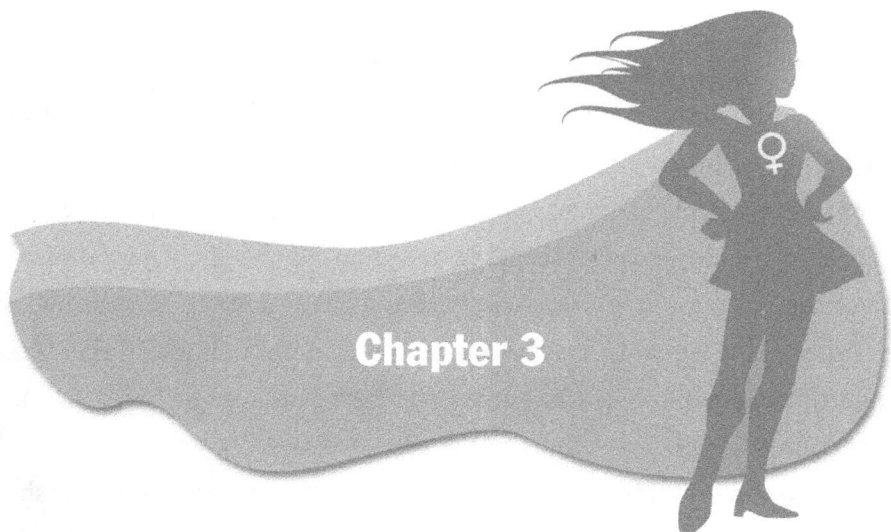

Chapter 3

Brave-ER - Face of Death

While growing up, there were only a few times that I could remember hearing about someone I knew who had died. In my mind, I equated death with the elderly. They say that only the good die young. However, when I was in high school, the sister of two of my good male friends was brutally murdered, which was so tragic because it occurred in the back of our apartment complex where we all lived. Her death affected everyone and it was creepy to find our family-oriented environment turned upside down into a crime scene. Yellow police tape was used to rope off the area where the murder occurred. The police officers questioned the majority of residence to glean additional facts that could be used to find the perpetrator.

My emotions were heightened too. I felt nervous every day that passed as the police looked for the killer. Like most women, I prayed that I wouldn't be the next to be raped and killed. The young girl's name was

Belinda. She was around sixteen or seventeen and a junior who went to my high school. She lived with her father and two brothers Tim and Terry. She and my sister were friends. They hung out with each other occasionally. However, it was her brothers and I who spent a lot of time together. I'd go to their house daily to hang out and watch TV. We had a good time joking around as we sat on their porch. Belinda's father was a hardworking man. He was hardly ever home because he had to work. His main goal was to put food on the table like many other single fathers caring for their children. Belinda worked too at a part-time job that she had to be at right after school. It was a local fast-food chain called Picnic Chicken. Their chicken reminded me of KFC's original recipe. It was pretty good. We get some for dinner now and then.

Our complex housed a few hundred low-income families. I knew most of the kids who lived there. We'd spend most summer days running all over the large complex while playing games like Hide And Go Seek, Tag, and Basketball. Back in those days, our parents yelled things like, "Quit running in and out of this house!" or, "Go back outside and play!" to keep us out of their hair. We didn't have the luxury of telling our parents that we preferred instead to stay inside to play video games as kids do nowadays.

The manager of our complex did his best to control the kids as it got dark out. He was a short Black man who had a rude demeanor. He didn't mix words while enforcing the curfew the parents agreed to when they signed their lease. He expected that all of the kids needed to be inside when the streetlights came on. He'd walk the entire complex with his large flashlight in one hand and fist clenched to enforce his curfew.

Parents would pay for violations of the curfew for not parenting their kids. He made them pay a fine. I made sure that I was inside because I didn't want to see those nasty black water bugs that came out at night to surround the inoperative swimming pool near the front entrance. There was a sea of them and it was gross. I hate water bugs and roaches.

I didn't have a choice when it came to respecting the curfew. My mother and the apartment manager would morph into monsters if I was late. I had no plans of disrespecting either of them.

In my mind, I equated death with the elderly. They say that only the good die young.

When the detectives found Belinda's half-clothed and limp body, it was evident that she had been beaten beyond recognition and had been raped. Everyone who heard the news wept, and it was a sad day. My first thought was, *Why would anyone do that to Belinda?* I wondered why her killer would perpetrate a heinous crime like that so close to her home. I believed that the killer was a monster. My heart broke for her father and brothers. It was difficult witnessing how distraught they were knowing that there wasn't anything I could do to help. After what seemed like weeks, the detectives revealed that they had apprehended her killer. They said that he was a disturbed man who suffered from mental illness. He lived in a nearby neighborhood with his parents.

The local news reporters said a man had been stalking Belinda. He knew her comings and goings since she had to walk past his house to get to work. On the dreadful day he murdered her, the killer followed her as she walked home and pulled her into the darkness of the back of our apartment complex where it was secluded. He raped and murdered her back there and no one heard her scream. It was reported that she had attempted to fight her killer but he was much stronger. Her death was a reminder of how our precious life can be taken in an instant.

Although there were warning signs for Belinda and it was probable that she knew her killer, there wasn't a lot that she could have done to stop a man with mental illness with bad intentions. Her death meant that women and girls in our community would have to be become brave-ER by having a greater sense of awareness when walking alone. We would be pressed to say something if we sensed something wrong no matter how trivial we thought it was. I adopted that strategy right away since my main mode of transportation was to walk everywhere I went. I was paranoid for a long time after Belinda's death. I was constantly looking over my shoulder and was afraid. However, I decided that I wouldn't allow myself to become so paralyzed that I allowed Belinda's perpetrator to control me. I realized that I needed to get to school safely. I also wanted to be strong for Belinda's brothers Tim and Terry who needed support.

Death struck close to me again, but this time it was too close. Being a mother of three small kids and still in my twenties, the last thing I needed to hear was that my husband had been murdered. We had been married for five years before he was gunned down and left to bleed out on a sidewalk in Harlem, New York. He was only twenty-seven. We were still trying to figure things out with marriage and parenting when he died. We'd watch TV shows like *Married with Children* for comic relief, but it didn't provide any practical solutions. My husband served his country in the United States Navy. He had been discharged a year before we relocated from San Diego to Newark, New Jersey. Once in Newark, we birthed our three children despite my husband's reluctance to have children. I was thankful that he gave me the gift of three beautiful children who I adore. Our oldest son was four and our twins were just a few days away from their second birthday when he was murdered.

It was on Friday the 13th when I received the news that I no longer had a husband and that my children would grow up without their father. He was a good dad who loved his kids. He was hands-on and playful. To have him taken from us so early in his life was something I wish hadn't happened. Our kids don't even remember him, which makes me sad. You don't realize how brave you are until you are put in a situation like that. That was the case for me. I kicked into survival mode to do what needed to be done. I didn't have a good support system, which forced me to be brave-ER in the face of my husband's death. My children needed me to remain present even though I was tasked with burying my husband. I was thankful that I was independent, which was a trait modeled to me by my mother. It was me against the world, and I was the only person who I could trust or depend on during that time.

As a teenager I was mature, and by the time I reached the ninth grade, I had earned the title of a "reliable babysitter". I babysat for friends of my mother and was able to secure a job or two on my own. I had natural motherly instincts that allowed me to connect with kids. I was an obvious choice, especially for those parents who didn't have a lot of money in their budget to pay for a babysitter. I was more than happy to help out when I could, but I quickly learned that babysitting could also be dangerous. I recall being asked to babysit for a family in my neighborhood. At the time, I was twelve years old and in the sixth grade. I played with their daughter Shannon. She was six years old. I didn't feel like I had a lot of options when it came to having friends in my neighborhood who were my age. I played with Shannon and another girl who was her age. I could either play with Shannon or hang out with my sister and her friends. They were teenagers who were interested in boys, smoking weed, and partying. Shannon's parents preferred that the older girls babysit Shannon's however, on one occasion they were out of options since the older teens weren't available. Shannon's father asked if I could help out even though it was an unusual situation.

I didn't know Shannon's parents too well, but I agreed to babysit after clearing it with my mother. To my surprise, Shannon's father tried to molest me. By the grace of God, he decided not to follow through with his inappropriate behavior.

> I kicked into survival mode to do what needed to be done. I didn't have a good support system, which forced me to be brave-ER in the face of my husband's death.

Before her parents left for their date, they provided me with instructions and their expectations. They suggested that Shannon go to bed at a designated time and encouraged me to watch television in the den. They permitted me to lay on the couch if I got sleepy. When Shannon's mother walked out to the garage, her father handed me a sexy nightgown that belonged to his wife.

"You can put this on later if you want," he told me.

I didn't know how to respond, so I nodded my head in agreement. I was twelve years old being told to put on a sexy nightgown. Shannon and I had an enjoyable time, and after she went to bed, I settled in the den to watch TV. Around 11:00 P.M., I decided to lay down on the couch and put on the nightie. I was naïve, so I didn't think I was doing anything that I shouldn't. To my surprise, Shannon's father returned home a little after 11:30 P.M. He claimed that he had left the party to come home to retrieve something he had forgotten. Before heading back out, he came into the den to check on me. I decided to play possum, believing that he would leave. I was wrong. He sat down on the edge of the couch to see if I was wearing the nightgown. I was nervous when I realized that he had bad intentions. He tugged on the covers, hoping to get a glimpse of me. I held on to the covers tightly. Once her father saw that his plan had failed, he left. I laid there shaken and wondering what to do. I realized that I needed to stay with Shannon until they returned home. They returned around 2:00 A.M., and after being paid, I quickly ran to my house that was two doors down. I vowed to never babysit for Shannon's parents and decided not to tell my mother.

I believed that not telling her was the best option. I had two options; the first was to not say anything, and the second was to tell my mother and have her make a ruckus in our quiet neighborhood. I didn't want my mother to assume that I had done something that I shouldn't have by putting on the nightgown. I wasn't going to take the chance of giving anyone a reason to play the blame game with me.

Those teen girls in my neighborhood continued to babysit for Shannon's parents and to hang out with her dad in their backyard while engaging in inappropriate conversations about sex with him. I wasn't going to be the one to blow the whistle. It made me feel sad knowing that Shannon's father was a pervert. I prayed that he wouldn't prey on her once she became a teen. I believe that I was brave-ER for not allowing the bogeyman to stop me from babysitting for others.

I quickly put the incident in the rear-view mirror. I began babysitting with a new sense of awareness. The next person I babysat for was a young single mother who lived in my apartment complex.

She needed a full-time babysitter. I was around fifteen years old when she hired me. She worked as a certified nurse's assistant. Her schedule required her to work long hours and to be away from her kids. Tina was her oldest child. She was five years old. The fraternal twins were named "Big Man" and "Little Man" and they were two years old. I established a close bond with her kids because we spent a lot of time together. I thought her kids were sweet, cute, and lovable. They confirmed that I had a knack for making kids feel safe and loved.

We spent an entire summer together. Our days were long but fun. They usually started at 6:00 A.M. We'd play outside, color, and one of my favorite things to do with them was to turn on the record player to listen to Aretha Franklin. They liked my singing. Before their mom would return home, I made sure they ate dinner, and I tidied up the apartment.

One of my less enjoyable duties was helping to potty train the twins. I realized that their mom needed my help. Overall, I had a positive experience and the pay was good. My time with them ended abruptly after my mother warned me that I was too young to be tied down with three kids. I agreed and quit. I spent the last days of my summer catching up with my friends.

My responsible and reliable traits carried over into other jobs. I either started in a leadership role or got promoted. For example, when I worked at McDonald's, I started as an assistant manager. When I got hired at the San Diego Zoo, I worked my way up the ranks and was promoted to run one of the many food concession stands. I loved working there and didn't have too many encounters with the bogeyman since it was a positive time in my life.

It took all those skills coupled with my being a mature young adult to be resourceful enough to come up with the cash to bury my husband. It wasn't going to be easy. I could either sit around whining or I could be brave-ER in the midst of the storm. I'm blessed that it was the latter. I was twenty-nine years old, a widow, and had three small kids to take care of. I had to push forward daily to make sure my kids were taken care of. I was working for a catering company at the time whose error placed me in a bad predicament. They dropped the ball by failing to activate my group insurance policy. Their failure caused me to scramble to come up with enough money for the burial services. I thought that I and my family were covered, but when I called to claim the death benefits, I was told that my policy hadn't gone into effect. There wasn't anything they could do about it. The company's Benefits Administrator had made the error of not completing the processing of my enrollment into the plan before going on sick leave. The company hadn't back-filled her job, which left my coverage in limbo. It wasn't a good time to be dealing with the issue. It wasn't helpful.

I was forced to figure out how to come up with a plan to come up with a few thousand dollars. I needed the money right away. The funeral home that I had decided to work with was a local family-owned business that was preferred by the community. However, they weren't sympathetic to my circumstances and told me they didn't offer flexible payment plans. I was stressed out. They made it clear, "No Money, No Services." I had a few days to come up with the money. I was frustrated. My deceased husband had plenty of friends and family, but not one of them offered to help me. Being brave-ER was a requirement in this situation. No one, not even the bogeyman, could stop me from making things happen.

My saving grace was to sell the one asset I had available. My husband's father had died a few months before him and left him with insurance monies. My husband took some of that money to purchase a vehicle. It was a Volvo that was in fairly new condition. I could generate some cash by selling it. As much as I needed reliable transportation, I realized that keeping the vehicle wasn't an option. It was a Godsend. God was my helper in so many ways during my husband's death. He was taking good care of me and the kids. We received some additional good news from the Newark Housing Authority. I learned that my husband and I had been approved for low-income housing. It was a blessing since I could no longer afford to pay the $800 rent for the condo that we lived in.

The letter from the Newark Housing Authority stated that I was assigned to one of the most notorious housing project in the city similar to the ones you hear horror stories about on television. This housing project was notorious for criminal activity, and gunshots could be heard in the middle of the night. I wondered how I and my kids would survive. However, God was with me. He assigned me to the building location in the front of the housing projects and had 24-hour surveillance by a Newark Police Officer. Me and the kids felt safe. Had I held on to the Volvo, it was likely that I would've been carjacked or worst killed for the vehicle. God allowed me to get money from the sale of the car to bury my husband.

My best friend Dee flew out from San Diego to Newark to support me. She and one of my husband's sisters were with me as I drove from dealership to dealership trying to sell the vehicle for a reasonable price. I decided to try to sell it back to the dealership where he purchased it. I hoped that they would have sympathy and treat me fairly. I was appalled by the salesman's attitude and his added insult to injury by telling me they would only give me half of the money they sold the car to my husband for. We hadn't owned the vehicle longer than a few months. I was determined to get more than half, but the other dealerships said the same thing. I was forced to settle for less although

I was furious. I hadn't expected to be ripped off. The disrespect caused me to feel sick to my stomach. I paid the balance of what I owed. By the time the funeral rolled around, I was running on fumes. I didn't have time to mourn my husband's death. It felt like a bad dream, but I was brave-ER in the days that led up to the funeral. Once things settled down, I spent the next few weeks moving into the apartment assigned to me. I was thrilled that my rent was drastically reduced to $200 and I wouldn't have to struggle to pay it. I couldn't wait for the funeral to be over so that I could shut the world out and to leave those behind who failed me during a difficult time.

> *I had the wherewithal to fight for what was owed to me. It's one of my bravest moments by far. God was with me the entire time.*

My next challenge was to hire a lawyer to represent me to get restitution from my employer for their error with the life insurance monies. I found the strength to be brave-ER in the fight. I was still employed by the company, so it took courage to work there while suing them. It took nearly two years for the company to settle. I was happy to win my case. I had the wherewithal to fight for what was owed to me. It's one of my bravest moments by far. God was with me the entire time. He protected me in the face of death. I learned that we have to keep fighting and that running off in the opposite direction isn't an option. I fought for my husband's dignity and memory by being brave-ER.

My final test of bravery in the face of death was to answer the call when a distant cousin called me with some bad news. I braced myself to hear what she had to say. She told me that my father had died. I felt the immediate urge to fly to Brooklyn, New York where he lived.

I wanted to attend his funeral. Being in his presence one last time was important to me even though we didn't have a relationship. I hadn't seen him since I was in the sixth grade, but I wanted to make peace with him once and for all.

I recall him asking my mother to meet him in St. Louis for what would be a mini-reunion back then. He and my mother had family in St. Louis and he wanted to spend some time with my sister and me. When my mother told us we were going to St. Louis, I was thrilled. It was the first time I would get to fly on an airplane. I also wanted to see my grandfather and my father. Throughout my childhood, I longed to be around my extended family. I felt lonely since it was just my mother, my sister, and me. We didn't have much contact with my extended family members who lived out of state.

Holidays, like Christmas and Thanksgiving, meant that it would feel lonely with it being just my mother, sister, and me together. We created our traditions, but I desired to be with more family members to build relationships. I often daydreamed about sitting around a large decorated table with aunts, uncles, cousins, and with the only grandparent I had alive to enjoy holidays. I hated the fact that I didn't know or have my family around. I found it to be a hard pill to swallow knowing that my father was part of a large family, which meant that my family was bigger than I could imagine. I was able to meet a few of his brothers and some cousins when we visited St. Louis when I was twelve. I was equally sad that I barely knew my father. It was rare to see any of my relatives so I was thrilled on the couple of occasions when my Uncle Carl and grandfather came to visit us at our home in San Diego. However, they didn't stay long enough for me to establish a bond with them.

I envied my friends who had grandparents and family who showered them with love in their lives. As a means to make me turn inward in times of despair, the bogeyman reminded me that I didn't have a lot of family on many occasions. He reminded me that there weren't many people out there who loved and accepted me. Although I knew that his narrative was a lie, the facts supported it. I chose to accept non-blood relatives who were willing to embrace me as their own, but it was only a temporary fix. I continued to feel that void until I had a family and could make some traditions that brought me joy.

My feelings of loneliness and my deep desire to have a relationship with my father caused me to search for him in my late forties. I believed that it was worth being rejected to reach out to him for an adult-parent relationship. We could take things slow and perhaps become friends. I used one of those online locator services to find him. Bingo! My efforts led to finding his sister who lived in Detroit, Michigan. She was a sweet lady who seemed happy to hear from me. She understood my plight and told me that she would help me get in touch with my father.

After talking to her for what seemed like a month, it was frustrating to hear the excuses she made for him for not calling me. I used the connection to learn all I could about my father. I wanted to get a sense of the man he was. She told me that she and my father had a close relationship and talked every Sunday. She promised to help facilitate our comfort level by reaching out to each other. However, for whatever reason, it took my father awhile to call me. The bogeyman made me question why he didn't want to get to know me. I pushed through the rejection and I didn't give up, so I kept calling my aunt and listening to her second-hand stories. She told me that my father loved my sister and me. I wanted a relationship with him so bad, and since he wasn't engaging with me, talking to her was the next best thing. I did my part to establish a relationship with her and drove down to Detroit a few times for in-person visits.

One day, out of the clear blue sky, my father called. I wasn't at home so he spoke briefly to my husband and left his contact information for me to call back. I called him back, and I had great anticipation that he would answer. A young boy answered the telephone, and I asked to speak to Clyde. The boy said that his grandfather wasn't home. He caught me off guard by his response because as far as I knew I didn't have any siblings. I remained cool, calm, and collected before asking the boy when his grandfather would be home. He provided an estimated timeframe for me to call back. I waited patiently to call him back. The first thing I wanted to know was if I had siblings. My father answered when I called back. We both seemed eager to talk. After getting the small talk out of the way, I asked who the boy was that had answered the telephone earlier. There was a noticeable pause before my father answered.

> The bogeyman made me question why he didn't want to get to know me. I pushed through the rejection and I didn't give up . . .

"He's my longtime girlfriend's grandson," he told me.

I was annoyed by his answer because I didn't think he was playing things straight with me. I probed more by asking how long they had been together and how many kids did she have. I asserted that my father was probably the only grandfather the young boy knew since the young boy had been living for so long with his grandmother, my father's common-law wife. I conveyed that I was happy for the boy and was willing to meet his family. I explained that I loved New York and had lived in New Jersey for several years.

I was curious, so I asked a final question, "Do I have any other siblings?"

"No," he quickly replied.

The bogeyman asserted that my father was a liar and that I should feel betrayed. However, I tried to remain positive and gave my father the benefit of the doubt. Regrettably, that was the last time I talked to my father. He never called me back or answered the phone when I called him. I believed that he was put off by my candidness. Who was I to question him about his relationships or if he had other children? I'm glad that I was brave-ER even if it meant he would dismiss me as his daughter. It was hard to accept the fact that he had rejected me in my childhood and was now making the choice to abandon me in my adulthood. This was his choice.

Sometimes in life, you have to accept the fact that you've done all you can to make peace with a mother, father, or other relatives. When they pass away, you don't have to feel guilty for not trying; that responsibility dies with them. God honors your willingness to forgive them and the efforts you made to establish a relationship with them. Keep in mind that you never have anything to lose when making the effort to repair a strained relationship, especially in a parent-child relationship. Sometimes things simply don't work out positively. When the parent dies, don't play the victim or the blame game with yourself. It's not good for your mental health or well-being. I was able to push through the negative thoughts I had about how our last conversation went.

I decided to honor my father by traveling to Brooklyn, New York to attend his funeral. My oldest daughter accompanied me for support. I reached out to my father's girlfriend after being given her contact information. She was gracious and provided me with the details for the service. She told me that she planned to add mine and my sister's names to the obituary and made sure she had the correct spelling of our names.

While attending the funeral, I studied my father's obituary and it was apparent that he had lied to me during our last conversation. The obituary listed a son who resided in Newark, New Jersey. I vowed to take a chance on getting to know my half-brother at a later date, but did entertain thoughts that it had been written there by mistake. It was a crushing reminded that my dad and I really didn't have a relationship. I barely recognized the eighty-something elderly white-haired man lying in the casket. I listened carefully to the stories from family members that were being told about my father. I learned a lot about his life as an army veteran and his years served as a civil servant. He was a mailman in his Brooklyn neighborhood. Everyone who spoke said beautiful and positive things about my father. I felt like a fly on the wall who had dropped in as a stranger getting to know a man who had helped give me birth. It felt awkward not being recognized or acknowledged by those who were his family. His common law wife had adult sons and daughters who loved him and had adopted him as their own dad. I realized that my father meant a lot to them and they grieved sobbingly for him. I was humbled by the experience. God allowed me to see that my father was a good man who I needed to forgive. I felt brave-ER because of my ability to provide grace while feeling disappointed.

BE Brave-ER

How do you offer forgiveness to a parent who disappointed you?

_____
_____
_____
_____
_____
_____
_____

How have you moved past hurts inflicted by a parent?

_____
_____
_____
_____
_____
_____

If abandoned by a parent, what is the story you tell yourself to overcome unresolved pain you feel?

_____
_____
_____
_____
_____
_____
_____

If you lost a friend at a young age to being murdered, how did you cope?

_____

_____

_____

_____

_____

_____

What are some practical things you can do to keep out of danger?

_____

_____

_____

_____

_____

_____

Chapter 4

Brave-ER - Release Judgement

Parents aren't provided with handbooks full of tips and advice on how to raise their kids. Parenting styles are subjected to and mirror the way a person was raised. Beliefs, values, and experiences are relied upon when interacting with our kids. Parents are left crossing their fingers and hoping their kids will turn out okay. The only evidence of that is successful adults who become respected and productive members of our society who can hold their heads high. They are willing to do whatever it takes to achieve what they consider success. A lot of parents use outdated parenting styles and ways of thinking. Frankly, these parenting styles are in desperate need of modification.

The way we parent our children is consequential. Our words and deeds, especially when angry, can be detrimental. When we show a lack of empathy, we are in danger of leaving our kids with deep scars that can result in damage that cannot be undone. The bogeyman loves to see parents make those mistakes because their behavior produces unruly kids who he can pick on too. We have to remind the bogeyman that our kids are not his to torture. We won't give up our peace by raising "bad kids".

When I was around six years old, I was a victim of unsympathetic words spoken to me by my mother. I'm sure she spoke them not knowing their effect and she believed she chose the right words at the moment. On that day, she was wrong. For the most part, I had an enjoyable childhood. I recall being a carefree kid whose only problem in the world was the fact that I felt lonely most of the time. My sister and I spent a lot of time playing outside. We'd stay outside for hours playing with the kids who lived in our apartment complex and neighborhood. Sometimes we'd take the liberty of venturing out to expand our territory. That's what kids did back then, and it now seems like things were a lot safer then. Parents didn't get ridiculed for not keeping a close eye on their kids like they have to do now. They didn't have to worry about a noisy neighbor sounding the alarm for them not watching their kids and calling the Department of Child Services on them for neglect.

We would walk to the store to buy candy. I liked having a few coins in my pocket to buy stuff. Now and then, I'd spend my money on something special for my mother to brighten her day. I'd walk into the local flower shop that was next to the store to pick out a single carnation for her. I couldn't wait to hurry home to give it to her. She'd be happy to receive the carnation while praising me for my kindness. I'd go back outside to play, feeling accomplished that I had a favor with my mother.

While outside, we'd explore the neighborhood and would end up going down into the nearby sewers. We wouldn't stay down there for too long, but it wasn't because bright flashing warning lights were letting us know that it wasn't a good idea to be lurking down there. We loved to play in the large hilly field that was nearby. We'd grab a piece of cardboard to slide down it. We had a blast.

> *We have to remind the bogeyman that our kids are not his to torture. We won't give up our peace by raising "bad kids".*

I assumed mothers back then were thrilled to get a few hours of alone time and peace while their kids played outside. It allowed them the opportunity to spend some quality time doing what they wanted to do to relieve some stress. By the time we came back into the house, my mother was usually in a better mood than she had been when we first went outside. As a parent, I understand why those breaks were needed. Parents have a lot to juggle.

One day, I was playing outside in the open area directly below our upstairs apartment, that is... until something terrible happened to me. I was in my little world and minding my own business. I must have been bored or didn't have anyone to play with. I noticed a vehicle pull up to park in front of our apartment complex. Two White males emerged from the vehicle carrying BB guns. I assumed that they wanted to practice shooting pigeons because I had seen people do that before. I heard one of them discharge his BB gun a few times, but I kept on playing. All of a sudden, I felt a burning sensation in my left eye. I realized that I had become their target by accident. I frantically ran upstairs to tell my mother what had happened. I wanted to be comforted by her. I knew she'd get an attitude with those men after hearing what had happened. She would have given them a good cussing out had she seen them.

My mother caught me off guard with how she responded to me, "What happen to you?" she demanded.

"Mama, those men shot me in the eye," I said while sobbing.

In my mind, it didn't seem like she had a sense of urgency to go after them. She asked for more details as she examined my eye. After determining that I wasn't in danger of losing my eye, she looked outside to see if she could find them. They had already fled after hearing me scream and cry.

"You shouldn't have been in the way," she warned.

My six-year-old self thought her response seemed cold. The moral of the story: Parents make mistakes with their responses sometimes. My goal isn't to make my mother seem like a bad mom. Her response was based on her parenting lens and what she knew to do at that moment. It's even plausible that someone in her life had dismissed her pain when someone put her in danger as a child. My mother had been raised by her father after her mother died when she was two years old. She was forced to grow up faster than most and often had to be the caretaker of her two younger brothers.

My mother had no idea that her words would remain in my head for years. I wore them like a badge of honor well into adulthood. They became my mantra and road map for how to navigate in my world. I'm sure you've heard your parents say similar things like, "Stay in a child's place," or, "You're a dumbass," or, "You ain't got no sense," and, "You're a fuck-up just like yo daddy."

Go ahead; be brave-ER by forgiving them. They probably had no idea that they were breaking your spirit with their words. Unfortunately, parents can't take their words back. Many of them don't realize that they're a trusted authority figure in your life who you are counting on to teach you how to survive in the world. Hearing the words, "You should not have been in the way," caused me to think about what she meant. I concluded that she was wrong to say that. Those young men were in *my space* and shouldn't have been in *my way* recklessly shooting BB guns while kids were playing outside.

Suddenly, I didn't feel safe in my own environment because of my mother's response. I had been minding my own business as I had been doing on so many other occasions. My mother's words hampered my self-esteem and caused me to go through life doing everything in my power to stay out of the way. I learned to hide, and as an adult, I hid in my house under the disguise that I was a homebody who preferred things to be this way.

The bogeyman had me in his clutches and I began to lose my vibrant light and love for laughter. I began to care way too much about what other people thought, said, and behaved. It bothered me that some envy me because of my material possessions, it was never my intention. It was hard living under the weight of those circumstances but I needed to be brave-ER. I held myself hostage in fear and minimized my professional accomplishments. I refused to drive my nice cars and didn't wear my beautiful jewelry when I was out and about. I played it small while shrinking until I barely recognize myself. I did it to make other people feel better about themselves. Perhaps my behavior sounds a bit insane, but I can say with certainty that I'm not the only woman who has ever behaved this way because they've lost their sense of self-worth.

We're all different, making our coping skills run the gamut. Some women turn to drugs, while others start sipping on their favorite wine every night until they find themselves masking the fact that they have turned into an alcoholic. We use all kinds of vices to drown the voices in our heads that are magnified by the bogeyman. I've learned to hide behind my smile. It helped me appear much happier while in public. I needed to be brave-ER. I began to embrace the idea of going to therapy but first I had to change my mindset about it. For many years I believed that therapy was for rich White people and I questioned if it worked. I thought it was worth a try since my insurance would pay for a few sessions.

Surprisingly, I was comfortable with the therapist assigned to me. I found her to be insightful and she provided me with some good advice to get back on track. During one of my session where she probed a little deeper, she asked for a response and I told her that I would try. She asserted that most people who use the word "try" before stating the action they plan to take are saying that they're choosing not to take any action steps toward their goals or plans because there is no "try" in taking action. You

> *I realized that I needed to start taking deliberate actions toward my goals and to stop worrying about what other people think about me.*

are either going to do something or you're not. I was trying to brave-ER, but my actions were failing. That was the turning point for me. I realized that I needed to start taking deliberate actions toward my goals and to stop worrying about what other people think about me. I shut the bogeyman down with tools like these.

Attending therapy was a positive experience for me. I benefited from it when I did the work. I found that when you don't address the things that keep you stuck in life, you remain immovable and sometimes even paralyzed. You wake up one morning to find that years have passed you by. You wonder why you haven't accomplished much more than you have already. God watched me place my dreams on hold and chuckled as I attempted to do things in my strength. I stacked my dreams in the corner like old newspapers waiting to be burned. I learned to turn to food to cope, and it wasn't long before I tipped the scale over 250lbs. I realized that I wasn't in control of my health or life. I didn't want to face my reality and fooled myself into thinking that since no one was calling me fat to my face perhaps I wasn't all that fat. A pretty face can only take you so far.

I learned the truth about my weight after reading some medical reviews. They indicated that according to my BMI, I was obese by medical standards. It was a hard pill to swallow. I was choosing to be an obese pretty woman who was married to a handsome man. My husband had married a much slimmer and healthier version of me. I'm not saying that it's not okay to gain some weight over the years, but what I am saying is that God created women to be the apple of their husband's eye, and we don't have permission to let ourselves go. The bogeyman convinced me to hide and allow other women believed they could lure my husband away from me since they weren't obese. This is the type of trickery he thrives for. "The Devil is a liar." I thank God that my husband never verbally complained about my weight or verbally abused me. He kept loving me though my weight gain while remaining my biggest cheerleader. He encourages me to be the best version of myself, and together we work on our health goals. I've since learned that my weight doesn't define me. Since weight is tied to our appearance, we have to pay attention to how we would like to show up in the world.

Adopting a new mindset can be tough, but I did it. I realized that I had value and did a mental overhaul consisting of therapy, saying daily self-affirmations, and practicing positive self-talk. I've also lost thirty pounds and plan to keep working hard to lose more weight. I'm a lot brave-ER these days. I've started driving my vehicles, wearing my jewelry, and I'm no longer hiding. God is my provider, and He gives me riches here on Earth. God wants me to share the good news with his people so that they can see that if He has blessed me, He can bless you. God continues to fill my cup and has provided me with the tools needed to live a bold life out loud.

BE Brave-ER

What is the one thing that you need to stop hiding from?

_____

_____

_____

_____

_____

_____

_____

What words of your parents that hurt you are you willing to finally let go?

_____

_____

_____

_____

_____

_____

Who have you allowed to stop you from being your authentic self?

_____

_____

_____

_____

_____

_____

What are some healthy practices you can adopt to become the best version of yourself?

_____

_____

_____

_____

_____

_____

_____

_____

_____

_____

_____

_____

Chapter 5

Be Brave-ER - Professional & Personal Relationships

May I let you in on a little secret? I've learned that having self-confidence is not only good for the soul, but you also have to safeguard it or you won't have much. Protecting your mind, will, and emotions are not just a good idea, it's a necessary part of self-care. When we fail to do it, the bogeyman shows up on the scene to make sure you'll continue to question your ability to gain self-confidence. The good news is that I've been sent to help you. God has chosen me to model change and growth through my examples to you. Now I admit that I've tolerated, suffered, and allowed the bogeyman to spook me, but I can also provide the evidence of how I defeated him too. My goal is to motivate you by holding up a mirror as a level of accountability for you. Self-reflection is good. I encourage you to stop doing what isn't working and start implementing a plan that will serve you well. I want to help you build some power and tenacity in your life. To achieve this goal, you have to address deficiencies so that you can reach positive areas of growth. I realize that it isn't easy, but it's necessary. Once we remove the barriers and can embrace the plan we have created for ourselves, we can begin to experience happiness in our personal and professional relationships.

Finding freedom in our work environment can be a daunting task and will look different for all of us. Wouldn't it be nice to experience serenity while at work since we spend the majority of our day there? Achieving freedom at work is fundamental to our happiness. We have to work hard to achieve it. The best way to start is to take inventory of our confidence in areas like our soft skills and the skills necessary to perform our work. In other words, are you confident in the work you do? We fail to do the work necessary to create happiness at work. We end up spending time working at jobs or in careers that don't serve our greater good.

This rings true for me as well. For example, I'm an author. Writing books and being creative is something I love doing. I've been able to pour my thoughts onto the pages to inspire my readership. It's therapeutic. One would assume that I would've sought a career as a writer or journalist. The truth is, I never considered it. As I began to find my footing as a writer, the bogeyman made me believe that it wouldn't pay the bills nor would being a writer get me any closer to becoming a New York Best Seller. My confidence in this area was lacking. When we aren't deliberate about the work we choose and we work at jobs that don't feed our passion, we don't experience freedom in the workplace.

There is something freeing about being a writer. I'm convinced that anyone can be one on a smaller scale. Everyone has access to a pen and paper they can use to journal their frustrations and to relieve some much-needed stress. Journaling is a great way to pour that best-seller that is living inside of you onto the pages of a journal. That complicated plot with all the twists and turns will cause the bogeyman to give you a standing ovation and to encourage you to go deeper into the chaos you have created.

However, the good news is that journaling makes the bogeyman feel threatened, because the more you commit to doing it, the less control he has over your life. You are doing the necessary work to be free of him. He prefers the old, the one always on the edge and living in a constant state of depression. Tame him! Get in the habit of carving out some time daily to journal your innermost thoughts and fears. Journaling permits you to have a brain dump without apologizing to anyone. It's the perfect tool for achieving freedom. Some of you have started journaling already and have bought into the value in it. Take a moment to imagine the added benefits that are the reduction of stress and the ability to be in a relaxed state.

> *Go ahead and be brave-ER by accepting accountability for yourself. It starts with honesty.*

Women tend to cower under the pressures that life brings. We've been taught to feel guilty for taking time out for ourselves and not appeasing our families, co-workers, and bosses. Taking on this added responsibility makes us feel weaker, and when conflicts arise, we can't handle them.

Choosing not to be brave is no longer an option. Go ahead and be brave-ER by accepting accountability for yourself. It starts with honesty. Tell yourself your truth, the whole truth, and nothing but *your* truth. Honesty is a gift that you can give to yourself. It's also a valuable example that you can model for other women.

I've had the pleasure of working for and with women in various times of my life. What I've found is that most women avoid conflict for whatever reason. It's become a standard operating principle. I'm also that way, depending on the circumstances. What I've learned is that you can also overcome avoidance by inviting God into the situation. He will help you resolve conflicts and find peace in the mess you've created. Stop hiding. We are so eager to throw in the towel at the first hint of conflict on the horizon. I realize that it's easier said than done because we don't always know where conflict is going to occur. We get ambushed by other peoples' problems and hidden agendas. Then they begin casting their aspersions on you, but we don't have to become a victim. Stop beating yourself up for allowing them to disrespect you. Be brave-ER by standing up for yourself. Do something about it!

There have been many days in my career when I've sat around complaining to a co-worker about another co-worker or a boss who drove me crazy. This is the definition of drama. I didn't handle the situation well, and I would allow my negative thoughts to fester until I felt like I was ready to explode. By the time I drove myself home and walked through my front door, I'd be angrier than I was when the incident first occurred. ALERT: Didn't someone mention that this is not self-care? Instead of winding down on the drive home and leaving the drama at work, I'd twist myself into a pretzel, forcing my husband to absorb my anger and all the details of my mess that meant nothing to him.

Keep in mind that this is spousal abuse. I'd go off on a tangent leaving out none of the details. From start to finish, I wouldn't be satisfied until he listened to everything co-workers had done to me. I never considered the fact that he could've experienced much of the same since he supervises adults that act like children sometimes. It's not fair to force our significant other to listen to conflicts that we aren't willing to resolve. I love my husband for listening to me even though he often tunes me out and nods his head in agreement at the appropriate time. I have him trained pretty well after twenty-eight years of marriage. I wish I could handle conflict the way he does.

My husband is straightforward and has a no-nonsense demeanor. I couldn't say half the things he does to solve conflicts, but he nips things in the bud in a timely fashion. I realize that I need to be brave-ER when dealing with conflict in the workplace. Allowing anger and resentment to drive a wedge between you and a co-worker or boss won't help you foster healthy professional relationships. Hurting co-workers' feelings or telling your boss where he or she can shove it might make you feel better temporarily, but it is not a lasting solution to effective problem solving. You have to watch your words in the workplace. Be brave-ER by adopting coping skills that work for you, and remember to be professional at all times.

Throughout my life, I've worked for bosses good and bad, however, I prefer to work with the ones that I deem to be good. God doesn't always give us what we want, but if we are willing to accept his correction, he will give us what we need. When I work for who I describe as a bad boss, a person who lacks people skills and is hard to please, I don't feel like I'm being my authentic self. They create a hostile work environment that causes me to feel stressed when I'm around them. I'm the opposite when I sit in the boss' seat. I pride myself on being genuine. I make every attempt to treat people fairly and the way I would like to be treated. I strive to ensure that they can meet their individual and developmental goals. I want them to thrive in a safe and positive environment.

When my boss knowingly or unknowingly creates a hostile work environment, I respond to the conflict that results from it based on my comfort level with them. The "A-Type" personalities are competitive, ambitious, impatient, and highly focused on the attainment of success.

To me, they will do whatever it takes to get to the next level, included trampling over others. I choose to hold on to my grievances with them. I allow conflicts to fester because I fear facing their aggressive demeanor and communication style. They make me feel like I'm being bullied. Bullying is a trigger for me that I avoid in order to guard myself. I assume that my boss will sabotage me and belittle my contributions to the organization. I conclude that they are spiteful for seeing me as someone who might get in their way of attaining the recognition they seek. Their perfectionist tendencies drive me crazy. They cast their aspersions on to my character when talking about me with others.

I respond by considering quitting my job or I picture myself kicking their ass in my dreams. These are thoughts and feelings courtesy of the bogeyman. He'd rather that I entertain negative thoughts than look for positive ways to address conflicts. I know I'm not the only one who deals with things this way. It is important to gain a sense of self-awareness. It is the only way to tame the bogeyman and to begin focusing on effectively managing your triggers and emotions while at work. Allowing your emotions to dictate how you behave is not a good practice and will not serve you well.

> *Bullying is a trigger for me that I avoid in order to guard myself.*

On the flip side, I prefer working for bosses with "B-Type" personalities. I'm in more of a relaxed state of mind and feel confident. I see eye to eye with them since I am also a "B-Type". They're tolerant of others and can resolve conflicts easier. I love the fact that they're assertive, relaxed, calm, and above all else — empathic. They don't ignite my triggers or make me feel like I'm constantly looking over my shoulder. I'm comfortable when communicating grievances and receiving feedback from them. They allow me to play it safe. It's better to be safe than sorry. However, playing it safe will not lead to growth opportunities or your ability to practice effective strategies while working with people who are different from you. This is where being brave-ER comes in. The good news is that God uses people to help us grow and develop. It's His way of stretching us. He wants us to be uncomfortable so that we can reach the next level of attainment that we desire.

We spend more time with our bosses and co-workers than we do with our families. That is why we need to cultivate relationships with the people and bosses we work with daily. This is a lesson that I had to learn. The "A-Type" bosses who I despised working with were placed in my life to serve as a conduit to get me to the next level. They forced me to address my shortcomings, my lack of assertiveness, and my fear of conflict. I learned that I am more than a conqueror. After embracing a new mindset, I found that my tolerance for working with different people began to increase. It wasn't my bosses who changed; I did. I embraced the needed changes. My ability to handle constructive criticism from "A-Type" bosses improved. I now feel confident in using my voice and speaking up about things that need to be resolved. My new mantra is that I have the right to speak if I perceive a threat on the horizon, and I honor myself when I do. "Ah-Ha" moments like these are necessary for our growth. Permit yourself to be brave-ER in your professional relationships. Be mindful of your shortcomings. Have confidence in knowing that you matter and what you bring to the table is worthy of being heard. You'll find peace amid the storm and will be proud that you've become brave-ER.

Our intimate relationships can leave us feeling empty, unsatisfied, and as if we're going insane. We become most vulnerable in those types of relationships because they are the ones capable of hurting us the most. We feel like we have to guard our hearts at all costs. However, there is a way to fix this and that is to build trust in your intimate relationships. You have to be willing to have honest conversations that detail your innermost thoughts and biggest fears. In other words, we have to let our significant others in by allowing them to experience our authentic selves. Many relationships fail because couples do the opposite; they hide things about themselves from the other. They don't even come close to scratching the surface to obtaining true intimacy. We find ourselves holding back because the bogeyman has convinced us that our mate can't handle our past. Our inability to trust is the culprit that holds us back. The issues stem from past childhood trauma. Without trust, it's difficult to maintain long-term, healthy, and meaningful relationships. Don't throw in the towel; there is hope to turn things around.

It's my believe that women fail miserably when it comes to trusting their mate. When we don't learn to trust, we often find ourselves feeling crushed under the weight of our world. We are tasked with wearing a lot of hats causing us to become exhausted from trying to juggle multiple roles. It doesn't help us that in the midst of it all we're trying to heal from our past hurts and betrayals. The bogeyman knows this and convinces us that we are better served by being shut down instead of trusting and engaging with our mate. The truth is, our significant other is probably managing a set of their own hurts, but when given the opportunity, they will rise to the occasion to help us be brave-ER. We don't have any valid evidence that they can't. By operating this way, we allow our joy to be stolen and we end up feeling unhappy and discontented. The thing we fear the most is being abandoned by our significant others. We decide to be in control by all means necessary, yet we are unable to hold on to the reins for long when we make that choice.

Would it surprise you to know that men are just as afraid as women are to fully trust while in intimate relationships? I learned this truth the hard way. Like many of you, I relied on the failed coping mechanisms that caused me to engage and to be presence enough to sustain my day-to-day intimate relationship. I simply wasn't leaning in or doing my best to nurture my relationship. I did my best with the skills I had to work with. When things started to fall apart, I sought the advice of everyone but my significant other. Actions like these do nothing to cultivate the intimate relationships we desire. If there is a snowball's chance in Hell for us to enjoy our relationship by correcting our bad behavior, we will have to be willing to take it. Learn a different approach while becoming brave-ER. Transparency is the key to successful relationships.

I'd like to share some of my failures and how I learned to prevail in sustaining a long-term, healthy, and loving relationship with my current husband of nearly three decades. With a great deal of humility, I can honestly say that the majority of our years together have been nothing less than harmonious. We had to do the work to make our marriage work. It required active listening and honesty. We threw out the old marriage manual that says that the stars have to line up perfectly to have a great marriage. Learning about your significant never stops.

I was like many other women who yearn to get married. It was high on my list of desires. I married twice after losing my first husband. I wanted to correct some of my wrongs from my first marriage, so I vowed to work hard the second time. I was eager to say, "I do," quickly and without hesitation. I couldn't wait to walk down the aisle in my beautiful wedding dress, something I didn't do the first time. As a child thinking about marriage, I had created the perfect picture for myself — I wanted to live in a house with a white picket fence, with two kids, and of course, a dog.

There are no perfect marriages! Let me repeat that. There are no perfect marriages, period! Now that I have your full attention, remember that thinking that they exist is faulty thinking. However, we do have the ability to create our version of perfect based on the things we cherish about our mates. Consequently, when my husband and I tied the knot, we started out withholding vital parts of ourselves from each other, believing that we needed to keep some things hidden until we could build up enough trust for the other to handle our story. Most couples behave this way. That's why it can take a lifetime to get to know each other.

As we worked on our trust, we agreed that we would take the "D" word (Divorce) off the table. We know people who use it in the heat of an argument or as an ultimatum. Respecting those boundaries has been a game changer for us. The "D" word is a loaded word and shouldn't be uttered unless you are serious and ready to get a divorce. The institution of marriage is not respected like it once was, so we have to work hard to preserve it. To succeed in marriage, you have to roll up your sleeves and do the work necessary to resolve marital issues. They will be complicated at best and will run the gamut. Divorce was never intended by God to be an option except in situations described in the Bible.

My husband and I have been brave-ER when it came to resolving conflicts. We worked to resolve them quickly. We also embraced the art of apologizing. I'm sure that sometime in your life you've heard that it's not good to go to bed angry at your mate, and I try not to.

God has demonstrated that he is the glue that holds intimate relationships together. He can be depended on to sustain marriages. He is masterful at turning things around no matter how bad they get. However, we have to invite Him in and reject the bogeyman. While growing up I wished that I had brothers, but since I didn't, my only reference for learning about male behavior was from the two men I married. Needless to say, they were different men, so I learned different things, positive and negative. However, they were good men who loved me without a doubt. I felt it deep in my soul. I learned from them how men think and how they process their thoughts. They are different from women. They say that men are from Mars and women are from Venus. I think there may be some truth in that statement.

> Contrary to belief, most married men love and adore their wives deeply above all else . . .

It wasn't until I walked into a local factory for work that I finally got the opportunity to experience the essence of male behavior. I was eager to learn all about it. The first lesson rang true to me. Contrary to belief, most married men love and adore their wives deeply above all else, notwithstanding the negative inferences that can be drawn from their behavior while working in a factory environment. You've heard some of those rumors about men flirting and touching women inappropriately. I found that to be true, even the fact that some men cheated on their wives with other women working in the factory. In fact, for some, the factory represented a supermarket of options to flirt with and to marry, divorce, and marry again. It doesn't matter what you look like or how you smell, if you're making that good factory money.

Stay with me; I'm going somewhere with this. You'll want to keep reading to hear all about what I was able to uncover. I worked around hundreds of men who looked nothing like my husband or the men in my family. They were White men of all sizes and ages. Nonetheless, some of them taught me a lot. I'm calling your attention to the men who come to work every day proudly carrying their oversized lunch boxes that are pack full by their wives. If you ask them about their wives, they speak highly of them and a conversation with them will go something like this:

"Hey, Ted, what are you doing this weekend?" you ask.

"Well, for starters, the wife has a "Honey-do-list" for me to finish up. After that, I'll probably mow the grass and catch the game," he'll reply.

The first time I heard Ted talk about this so-called "Honey-do-list", I was floored. I wondered what the hell one looked like. I couldn't believe that Ted, after spending hours working in the factory all week, would be willing to commit to doing work all weekend around his house. He would even mow the lawn to please his wife. Let's just say that I was a bit surprised since I hadn't had the benefit of growing up with a father in the home. This so-called "Honey-do-list" was a new phenomenon to me. Then my faulty thinking kicked in and made me question Ted's actions. Since Ted was White, I wondered if "Honey-do-lists" were only handed out to White men by their White wives. Let's face it; my husband worked hard at the factory every day just like Ted, but he had never brought up to me the notion that there was a "Honey-do-list" and I could have one. Perhaps it was because my husband's idea of a "Honey-do-list" was "Honey, I done worked twelve hours each day this week and took out the trash cans on Tuesday."

See how the bogeyman will play with your mind and make you feel like your less than or missing out on something. What I gleaned from analyzing this situation was that the only difference between Ted's wife and me had nothing to do with lunch boxes, but more about the way Ted's wife simply asked him for what she wanted. They had good communication skills and she met Ted's needs. Ladies, that's the secret to a happy marriage. Each partner taking care and being fully present with the other. Ted's wife asked for what she wanted and Ted was happy to oblige.

After learning the art of the "ask", I continued to observe Ted and others like him. Unknowing, they were teaching me how to use my voice and how to speak to the heart of my husband. I was gaining favor with him from the lessons and grabbed ahold of every lesson they taught me. I didn't allow them to escape my memory. Lesson #1- Stop withholding love or anything else from your husband. Lesson #2- Be willing to demonstrate a love that surpasses understanding in the good and the bad times. Love your husband with your entire heart. It was a great study. Tip after the tip was being given, but then, Ted pulled out a bonus tip that caused my ears to perk up when I listened to his answer about his upcoming vacation. It was something along these lines:

"Hey, Ted, what are you doing on your vacation?" I asked.

"Well, the wife and I are going shopping for a new stove and refrigerator. She's been on me about shopping for them and remodeling our kitchen. I should've gotten the job done a long time ago, but I'll complete the work in a few weeks."

I thought to myself, *Say what!*

Ted was showing his butt. However, I leaned in to pay close attention to all the details. I knew I would be giving myself some homework. I decided to try this tip out on my husband. I wanted some of the same things Ted's wife wanted. The reason I wasn't getting them was that I hadn't asked. At that time, my husband and I had lived in our house for over twenty years. Investments like these were well overdue. It never occurred to me that getting a new stove and refrigerator was only an "ask" away. I didn't hesitate to ask for them.

His response blew me away when I said, "Hey, love, I heard one of the ways a husband can show his wife love is to buy her a new stove and refrigerator," I reported.

"Unhun," he replied.

I realize that my "ask" seemed a bit manipulative, but not only did my husband buy me a new stove and refrigerator, but he also told me that I could expect to have my kitchen remodeled in the next couple of years. He was more than happy to oblige and to make me happy. Husbands, no matter the color of their skin or length of marriage, want to make their wives happy. A happy wife equals a happy life. However, husbands aren't mind readers, so wives have to be brave-ER by asking for what they want. I quickly got busy with making a "Honey-do-list" for my husband so that he could address all of my wants around the house. Guess what? It worked!

The moral of the story isn't for you to do a shakedown on your husband to get him to purchase material things, or for you to put him on a guilt trip for not performing those much-needed repairs around the house. It's a little more complex than that. I relate it to learning to bring your authentic self to the table when engaging with your mate.

> *A happy wife equals a happy life. . . . so wives have to be brave-ER by asking for what they want.*

It's important for you both to actively work on being transparent to help the relationship to flourish. Refrain from withholding things like sex, money, feelings, dreams about the future, and "ask" to make you happy. Remember that it's important to talk about your mutual goals, but even in marriage, individual goals are important too. They should be evaluated regularly and worked on. I also learned that it's about feeding the soul of a man and having him feed your soul too. We can honor each other by asking for what we want with clear expectations.

Here's the best takeaway that I can offer: Men want to please their wives and they care about their happiness above all else. After being schooled by Ted, I was able to move forward and to stop believing the lie the bogeyman was feeding me that White men are the only ones who are willing to go the distance to make their wives happy. I can't tell you how happy I was to see my husband's willingness to oblige me. To date, he makes me feel special every day.

The Bible teaches us that wives should pray for their husbands daily and make them feel like they're the most important person in the entire world. I edify my husband daily and make a point of telling him how much I appreciate him. I love seeing his handsome face and bright smile as he embraces my new way of engaging with him.

Our love has been strengthened by our improved communication. My husband has shared the secret to a long and healthier marriage with his close friends. Some have taken his tips and run with them, while others believe that sticking to the status quo works best for them. By now, I hope that you're feeling all warm and fuzzy and busting at the seams to put these tips to work. I encouraged you to be brave-ER and do so right away and remember to be your authentic self and you'll see a noticeable difference in your relationship.

Since I'm on a roll and sharing with you my great tips, I would like to share yet another lesson. I worked for a man who I thought had it all together. He and his wife went on vacations to Hilton Head, where he'd golf and his wife and kids sat on sandy beaches with the bluest of waters rushing to the shore. Occasionally, his wife would stop by the office to see him. There was one thing about her that always caught my attention and impressed me. My boss' wife wore a huge five-carat diamond solitaire on her ring finger. I was dumbfounded since I had never seen a "normal" person who wasn't a celebrity wear such an amazing diamond ring.

"Wow! My boss must love his wife," I said to myself.

Okay, I know you're thinking that a diamond's size shouldn't equate to a man's love for his wife. However, I beg to differ in some cases; it is the way men magnify their love and put it on display for the whole world to see. This took me back to thinking about what Ted in the factory had taught me, and once again my quandary led me to test another hypothesis. I wanted to know if White women were the only ones who could get their husbands to purchase diamonds larger than a carat for them. I wanted one but thought that I was being selfish if I asked for one since the wedding ring I had made me happy.

Let me take a moment to clear things up: Black men do, will, and can afford impressive diamond rings and will purchase them for their wives. I know this to be true because I have the receipts; my husband is one of them. However, his thinking was different from my boss in how he valued diamonds and his belief that a man should get it right the first time and purchase a diamond his wife will love and will make her happy for the duration of their marriage. My husband believed that if those steps were taken, there wouldn't be a need for a future upgrade.

When we first got married, I was happy to receive the beautiful marquise diamond that he purchased for me. It was lovely. Since we had been married for some years, after seeing my boss' wife's ring, I wanted an upgrade. I began bragging about my boss' ring choice to my husband. I claimed that he must love *his* wife to buy her what looked like over a five-carat solitaire. I wondered if she had been a better wife than me or if there was some special dialogue or action I was missing to get one like that.

Little did I know, my husband was taking in all of my subliminal messages and he was processing them. Subconsciously I desired a larger diamond, but like with the stove and refrigerator, I wasn't willing to use my voice to ask for what I wanted. I began telling myself that I wasn't deserving of one. "You are what you think?"

My husband is a good man who loves me. To my surprise, many years later, my wish for an upgrade materialized. My husband gave me not one but two impressive diamond upgrades. The second one was mind blowing! I received the upgrade about six years ago. I recall us walking into a local jewelry store. We went there with the goal of window-shopping and to get my wedding ring cleaned. While in the jewelry store, the owner, who knew us because we were regular customers, asked if we wanted to see a custom-made white-gold diamond ring that had three welded diamond bands. I was excited to see the masterpiece.

When she pulled the ring out, I looked at it in amazement while trying it on. The beautiful ring fit perfectly. After what seemed like a minute or two, my loving husband said he was buying it for me. I nearly fainted. I got the upgrade I wanted and it was beyond my expectations. The lesson I learned in this scenario was that White men aren't the only ones willing to magnify their love visually with large and impressive diamonds. Men shell out thousands of dollars to purchase big shiny diamonds, not because of their ego, but because of their desire to oblige and please the women they love. It's a heart and "ask" thing.

How do you make them feel, and how do you reciprocate their love? All men want the world to know that they are committed to you and you're committed to him, and the best way to do that externally is to have you wear his impressive diamond wedding ring on your finger.

I want to make myself clear: There is no way I'm suggesting that your marriage is in trouble if you're not wearing a big shiny diamond on your finger, or your kitchen has yet to be remodeled, or you desire to have a new stove and refrigerator.

WARNING: These are my asks of my husband. In other words, the things that I desired and would make me happy included a "Honey-do-list". They just happened to be the same things that the men who taught me the lesson of "asking" said that their wives wanted also. They were important and specific to me. Because we are all different, your desires will be different and unique to you. The moral of the story is that you have to ask your husband for what it is.

Remember, husbands aren't mind readers, and you can't fault them for not giving you what you're not willing to ask for. That's how it works. Don't ask your husband for things because other women have them, like bigger diamonds. You might desire some simpler things, like being taken on a romantic vacation, getting a new car, having a long break from the kids, partaking in a two-hour massage, or taking a nap in the middle of the afternoon. The moral of the story is: *You don't have what you want because you haven't asked.*

If you are feeling stuck and unable to have an honest dialogue with your husband, lean in; you can turn that around today. Demonstrate that you love your husband with your entire heart and let your actions reflect your love for him. Be transparent and ask for what you want. Be sure to have clear expectations. Your happiness and ability to enjoy a healthy and loving long-term marriage depends on it.

BE Brave-ER

What workplace conflicts do you need to address?

_____
_____
_____
_____

How do you address contentious situations with your boss?

_____
_____
_____
_____

Can you demonstrated confidence in your abilities when using your voice to advocate for yourself?

_____
_____
_____
_____

What approaches have you taken to strengthen your relationship with your significant other?

_____
_____
_____
_____

What would it take for you to give your entire being to you husband or significant other?

_____
_____
_____
_____

What is your current ask of your husband?

_____

_____

_____

What are some ways you can be brave-ER by when asking for what you want?

_____

_____

_____

How can you be transparent with others when sharing your past so that you can be supported?

_____

_____

_____

What strategies can you use to fight fair with your significant other?

_____

_____

_____

What tools can you provide your significant other with to help them face obstacles?

_____

_____

_____

How can you incorporate apologizing into your method of resolving conflicts when they occur?

_____

_____

_____

Chapter 6

Be Brave-ER Self-Development

I AM Worthy. I AM Beautiful. I AM Talented. I AM Loved. I AM Remarkable. I AM Enough. I AM Brave. I AM Resilient. Hearing yourself repeat *"I AM"* affirmations are powerful! It is also a great way of building self-esteem. The more you repeat these affirmations, the more you will begin to accept them as truth. This will help you to build up equity in the bank of self-love. You'll be making "positivity deposits". These healthy deposits will serve you well, especially on those days when the bogeyman has accomplished his goal of taking you out. He will make you feel defeated and make you feel as if you can't take another step. Commit to saying affirmations that are meaningful to you for at least ten minutes a day. As you develop this habit, your "positivity deposits" will increase. You have to build yourself up. The keyword is: You have to do it and you can't depend on anyone but you. It's YOUR responsibility!

What you think about and tell yourself about yourself will be obvious to others and could be detrimental to you. Your thoughts are reflected through your actions and how you express yourself in the world. God reminds us that we are beautifully and wonderfully made. We should believe it. God uses millions of adjectives to describe us because we are precious to HIM. Allow Him to lead you toward the goal of self-efficacy. This will lead to increased self-confidence. We have to get busy and start doing the work to develop into a brave-ER and beautiful best version of ourselves.

In 2017, I was on the highway that was leading me to improved self-development. There were a lot of great things happening for me in my personal life. God was trusting me with more favor and abundance as an entrepreneur. However, the bogeyman continued to abuse me and to remind me of my failure with losing weight. I had a goal of fitting into a little black dress that I believed would define my success and self-approval. I desperately wanted to wear one and to put on a pair of stilettos with red bottoms. I could have this look, and my husband would be more than willing to purchase the sexy dress and shoes for me at a moment's notice. I counted myself out based on my failure to make my body look like it once did.

I got lucky when God sent a good friend my way to help me out. She stepped in to tag me back into the game. She asked me to attend the women's event she was hosting. I was already a published author with three book titles under my belt. However, I was stuck and had stopped marketing myself with the same vigor as I did in 2012 when I launched my first book. It was a great time, and my confidence was at an all-time high. I was seeking and securing radio interviews to talk about my book Addicted to Dysfunction: Released to Live Life Out Loud.

Similar to my friend, I wanted to make my impact in the world and to impart wisdom into the hearts and minds of women. I needed her push and the support she was providing me. I felt like a bird using its wings for the first time and was becoming comfortable in my skin.

I attended her women's event, and while there something sparked my love for connectivity with like-minded women. I began attending women's conferences across Indiana and out of state as well. I began surrounding myself with positive women whom I admired and were heading in the direction that I wanted to go. They were my teachers. My willingness to break free from my comfort zone was paying off. I realized that I had the "it" factor like other trailblazers I knew. My bravery was tested when an organization in my city hosted a Little Black Dress event. Had I not been putting myself out there, attending the event would've been out of the question. However, I went out and brought a black dress that wasn't so little. I committed to attending the event. I looked great in my dress along with the basic pair of black pumps I decided to wear. I felt fabulous. It didn't matter what size I was or what I was wearing while being surrounded by women of all shapes and sizes. I had a blast and had no regrets about attending. I was brave-ER. It's called growth.

> *I began surrounding myself with positive women whom I admired and were heading in the direction that I wanted to go.*

I have learned to remove the limitations that, courtesy of the bogeyman, had been placed on me. My gifts and purposes were on display, and I was receiving support from other women. I enjoyed hearing their feedback and how my book was changing lives. God was confirming that I was walking in the purpose He had given to me. I wasn't sitting on the sidelines or spending too much time strolling through Facebook, which can be toxic for me. The confidence I had gained reminded me of my younger self, back in high school, running around in my cheer uniform. I was experiencing joy and my confidence was through the roof. The wind was at my back and I soared like a beautiful butterfly over the fields. I felt energized as the sun shined on my face. I realized that I could do anything through Christ who strengthens me, and I felt proud that I was being proactive instead of reactive.

Over the next few years, I stayed focused and I planned impactful moves toward helping myself to live a purposeful life. I experienced one of my bravest moments when I decided to host my first women's conference. It took guts to organize it since there were already some trailblazers in my community doing the same thing. I loved the fact that they weren't afraid to roll up their sleeves by taking on leadership roles. God reminded me that there was more than enough room at the table for all women and that it was *my* time. Women were waiting to experience my impact on the world.

I purposely named my conference after my first book: The Release to Live Life Out Loud Conference. I wanted to demonstrate how women were living by that mantra and weren't afraid to go into business. I provided women with a platform to share their inspirational stories, a showcase marketplace for services, and to recognize a few phenomenal women for their excellence. It was a great conference. My husband, twins, and a handful of special friends helped me to make it a reality. I felt brave-ER knowing that I had utilized new skills that I allowed to be hidden. I manifested the conference that I had dreamt about it. It was a boss move! My actions led to having an annual event, but Covid impacted the 3rd annual event. I canceled it as the pandemic rushed in to shut down our world. The pandemic forced a lot of women, including me, to take a deeper look at ourselves. We went to great lengths to re-invent ourselves.

Can we talk pandemic? What a horrible time in our history. It was tough on everyone, especially women. Many of us mourned the death of friends and loved ones who would never get an opportunity to see their full potential. If you lost someone or had to deal with having Covid, may God bless you. A lot of women embraced the quietness the pandemic forced on us. They say that out of the darkness comes the light. In this case, the light was many new businesses and newfound talents. Some women lost their jobs and were forced to home-school their kids. God knew that no matter what, we could handle it, and that is why He has provided us with that extra bit of strength that we can lean into when needed.

It was a dark time and a difficult time. Many of us learned just how resilient we are. We refused to quit, and even in the most difficult times, we tapped into our gifts.

2020 was a mix-bag for me, full of emotions and opportunities to grow. I was successful in some areas, and in others, not so much. I believe that I was one of the lucky ones because I was allowed to work from home for the better part of a year and a half. My team wasn't considered essential workers. I spent the majority of my time inside the house, especially during those early days. Initially, my husband worked from home but was forced to work every day. His employer quickly implements safety protocols from Covid for the workers. For the most part, the plans were successful.

I'd wake up every morning feeling more comfortable being able to work from home. I'm somewhat of a homebody anyway, so being in the house felt safe during all of the chaos. However, as time passed, I began to feel like a hermit, causing some depression. Before the pandemic, I was riding an ultimate high by traveling all over the United States to visit my children, hear some great comedy, enjoy a great concert, or attend some type of women's event. Suddenly, all of these things were taken from me and I was no longer in control.

At the beginning of 2020, I wanted to work on my development, so I enrolled in two programs. The purpose of one was to finally complete my Master's Degree in Business Administration. It was a long time coming since I had started the program back in 2005, and by this time I only needed to complete two classes. The bogeyman tried to convince me that it wasn't worth the trouble since I probably wouldn't have an opportunity to use the degree so late in my career. However,

> *God stepped in and reminded me how important it was to finish what I started.*

God stepped in and reminded me how important it was to finish what I started. I also enrolled in a program to become a Life Coach. I had desired to become a Life Coach for years, and it was something near and dear to my heart. I've spent my entire life coaching others. I was happy to be able to finally complete both of these goals in 2020.

Being forced to be at home due to the pandemic meant that I would get a lot of my time back since I wouldn't have to travel back and forth to work. My job required me to drive to different counties for meetings across the whole state of Indiana. I would also save a lot of money not having to pay for gas or unhealthy lunches daily. I took pleasure in shopping online at Amazon like everyone else. I began to accumulate a lot of new things that were on my wish list.

In the summer of 2020, I was proud of myself for being disciplined and completing both programs consecutively. My hard work paid off and I was awarded my professional coaching license and my MBA. I wanted to share my accomplishments with friends and family and to be celebrated by them. However, because of the pandemic, I couldn't. Indiana Wesleyan University informed me and the rest of the 2020 graduates that we wouldn't be able to experience a traditional commencement ceremony. Instead, they would be hosting virtual graduation some months later. I felt disappointed. Completing my MBA and being able to walk in the ceremony with my distinctive cap and gown was important to me.

The bad news weighed on me, but I had no choice but to get over my disappointment. A virtual graduation option wasn't going to fulfill my needs. I considered throwing myself a graduation party and taking pictures in my cap and gown, but when I didn't, it added to my sadness. The bogeyman egged me on in my lack of ability to celebrate myself.

A few months later, I began to feel distracted, inattentive, and unmotivated. I wasn't making any progress professionally or personally. I asked myself how I had allowed myself to go downhill so quickly. I didn't want to do anything. I realized that my distractedness was directly linked to my limited social engagement. I was also consuming too much news (news junky over here) as a means of staying abreast and connected to the chaos that had taken over our world. I wanted to stay informed about the climbing number of Covid deaths and to find answers as to when this nightmare would be over.

It was also around the time when the world stopped due to the racial inequities with George Floyd. Things had gone viral and people all over the world were protesting police violence. The details surrounding his death were hard to watch and hear, but like others,

I couldn't look away. It was a stressful time, to say the least, and I felt like I had taken on more of the world's pain than I could endure. I didn't realize that my over consumption of bad news was making me sick. I was forced to address this issue and to admit that I had become depressed. On some days I didn't have the desire to get out of bed. I needed help to cope, so I sought the help of a professional therapist to work with me on an individual basis.

Life is hard. No one said that it would be easy, especially when we feel like we have lost control over the things we feel we should be able to control. It seemed like 2020 was laying layer on top of layer to burden me.

My husband and I moved in 2020. We were excited to have built a house during the pandemic and were now moving into our new neighborhood. Our neighbors are mostly White, which added some additional stress to our lives because of the racial strife occurring in the world.

We began building our home in early 2020 and noticed that our neighbors seemed gracious, sweet, and welcoming when we came over to check on the process that was being made on our house. We loved the fact that we would be living in a lively neighborhood where its residents rode bikes, walked the neighborhood, and engaged in friendly conversations. It was a bonus and I felt grateful to live in an environment like that.

However, after the racial injustices were being covered on the news and across our newspapers daily, our neighbors seemed uncomfortable in our presence. They weren't waving as they had and many turned their heads when they saw us. I hated my new reality and wished things weren't that way. I can report that after some time passed some attitudes shifted and things are much better now. I had to push through a lot of things in 2020. My husband reminded me that I needed to brave-ER while pushing through and working on my mental health and self-care.

In addition to being closed off from the world and not being able to see my children or my new granddaughter who was born in late 2019 caused me some depression as well. It seemed like I had lost all of my essential connections in an instant, including relationships with the women in my circle. I thank God that I was able to get some wins to celebrate during the pandemic.

One was the fact that I began to tame the bogeyman after he tried to convince me to eat my emotions. He tried to push me over the edge by telling me that it was okay to eat entire packs of double-stuffed Oreos while having to stay indoors. At first, he succeeded as we were making food runs and Oreos were on the shopping list at least a couple of times per week. It was easy to eat them since they tasted so darn good. After feeling guilty and ashamed, I was able to stop myself.

In late August of 2020, God spoke to me and pressed upon my heart to be exercising and focusing on my health. It was the only way to address my weight. God also told me to add addressing my mental health to the list too. I listened, and it wasn't hard to get my buy-in since losing weight and being healthy was something I desired.

The first step for me was to contact my insurance company to get a referral to see a therapist. When I found one who I wanted to work with, we agreed that I needed to attend bi-weekly sessions. My therapist helped me realize that I needed to experience a mind shift. My current way of thinking was faulty. I'm grateful that I took action and followed God's much-needed advice. Once I began to establish a routine, I received a second download from God. He placed in my spirit the idea to become a physical trainer. At first I dismissed the notion. The bogeyman taunted me and asked if I was the right messenger to encourage others since I was obese. But God said I was the right messenger and becoming a physical trainer would allow me to learn about the body and bones and how they work.

He told me that if I understood the benefits of exercise and its correlation to preventing diseases, I would be able to become brave-ER in my fight to be healthier. He reminded me that since I had a platform, I could help other women in this area and that I didn't need to be 125 lbs to make an impact. I agreed. Being healthy is a tool that will allow me to communicate everything that God wants to flow through me and to women. Being a healthy vessel will provide me with the confidence needed to attract the women God wants me to serve. I have embraced the idea and am taking one step at a time to achieve my health goals.

I started out exercising a few days per week with my preferred mode which is walking. I began to walk for longer durations and felt blessed that I didn't have to modify my routine in the winter since I could get my steps in the privacy of my home. When started, I could consistently get in 2,000 steps and now I'm able to get 6,000 when I'm being intentional.

I'm enjoying reaping the benefits of walking too, which have been feeling more energized and my clothes fit better. To date, I've lost thirty-two pounds. My goal is to continue on this healthy journey and to lose an additional forty-nine pounds. I continue to study for my physical trainer exam. They say it's one of the hardest tests to pass because there is a lot of information to learn about different exercises, how the body works, and the professional protocols for physical trainers.

It's important to me to be healthy no matter how much the bogeyman attempts to distract me with reasons to be in social settings with delicious foods. My goal is to combine my coaching disciplines so that my clients can have a well-rounded coach who desires to help them live their best lives.

I turned sixty in the summer of 2021. It's yet another milestone birthday that screams, "It's never too late to learn something new." However, no matter your age, you can't escape the bogeyman. He'll rear his ugly head and remind you that you're getting old and that old people become less relevant over time. That's the lie he's been telling me. I decided to share my feeling of anxiety about turning sixty with my husband.

> *Sharing your deepest thoughts and fears with your husband is necessary so that he can support you.*

Note: Sharing your deepest thoughts and fears with your husband is necessary so that he can support you. It's part of your continuous bonding with him to gain his favor and to enjoy a healthy long-term marriage. My husband seemed surprised by my confession.

He encouraged me in the moment, "Babe, just keep working. It doesn't matter how old you are. You still got it, baby," he assured me.

"I'm afraid I won't be relevant anymore, but I refuse to take myself out of the game again," I admitted.

My fears were real. It wasn't so much about the number sixty than it was me recalling all that I had gone through to get there over the years and who I would become moving forward. I feel blessed that God has allowed me to live this long, but I also realize that I'm closer to dying than I was at the age of thirty. As I continue to age, I desire to do more amazing things and want to be seen as a trailblazer. I don't want to die until I've accomplished my purpose in its totality. I want my reach to be magnified and more impactful than it has been in years past. To accomplish these goals, I have to be healthy with a sharp mind. The bogyman keeps whispering in my ear, "The older you get, your memory, mobility, and energy will fade."

Although many of these things are true, I plan to prove the bogeyman wrong. I will be intentional about working on my mind, health, will, and energy. I hope to be a senior citizen with a zest for living. I want to reenforce the notice of relevance in other people my age.

Do you remember how, back in the day, people purposely sought the guidance of their grandmothers for wisdom? She had those valuable anecdotes and teachable moments to share. Many families wrote them down and they were passed on to the next generation. I want to be that grandmother, teaching millions of teachable moments not just for my family but for women of all ages. Remaining relevant is worth the fight. I don't want to end up being like Stella, struggling to get my groove back. I will make my mark that will last long into the next few decades. That's what is important to me.

When I turned fifty, I had similar thoughts as I do with sixty. I wondered how being fifty would make me feel and if I would be relevant. I was afraid then too and didn't want to get old. It seemed like my fifties went past quickly. However, what I learned was that I was relevant throughout every one of those years. I even heard from others that fifty was the new thirty and I was beginning to buy into this notion. My late fifties were some of my best years. It seemed like my circle of influence had grown and to become an entrepreneur was a blessing that brought me incredible joy. Of course, there were plenty of life lessons to learn, but I embraced learning so that life wouldn't pass me by.

Some lessons I had to learn repeatedly. However, I was able to change some of the behaviors that were no longer serving me. While in therapy, I learned some valuable coping skills that revealed more about who I am and what I'm capable of doing. I began addressing my health and my ability to admit (in my own words) that I was depressed and obese. Being obese based on medical standards is something that I didn't want to comprehend. I learned not to worry too much about being judged for my obesity after saying it out loud. I've learned to celebrate wins both big and small and continued to live my life out loud. My mantra is, "If I did it before, I can do it again." I'm taking this freeing mantra with me well into my sixties. If I'm successful in my sixties, then that means I can take that success with me well into my seventies and eighties. That sounds delightful, if you ask me. The key to doing so is to stay focused and never stop being intentional. I'm in control of my mind, will, and emotions. It has helped to keep the bogeyman at bay. I've learned that the only person who can stop me is me.

You have to be self-aware and able to recognize your strengths and opportunities at any age. I recognized that one of my opportunities was to become more proficient with technology. It's hard keeping up with those tech-savvy millennials. I have to remain open-minded and not entertain thoughts of throwing in the towel and being impatient. I have to hang in there until I catch on. I'm committed to being a lifelong learner, knowing that if I don't, the world will pass me by. Having awareness like this will keep me relevant and can help to serve my greater good. My purpose is to continue edifying women. I love watching them become change agents. Keep in mind that women are powerful and there are so many people relying on what it is that you bring to the table, so work on your gifts and display them at all times.

The more you do for yourself, the more God will partner with you to help perfect your gifts. God blew me away this year when He provided me with a professional mentor. I can't think of a better way to remain relevant. I needed a professional business mentor, and the one He sent me is awesome. God sent him through a woman I met at an online women's event. She shared with me how I could get a mentor for free by graciously referring me to a service that provides professionals with business mentors.

My mentor has been a Godsend. He has provided me with great tips to help me launch my professional coaching business the correct way. I appreciate his business acumen and experience in the business. I love the way he challenges me to see myself bigger, and I can't wait to reap the benefits.

> *The more you do for yourself, the more God will partner with you to help perfect your gifts.*

God is preparing me to become a savvy business professional and life coach. I want to be the same thing to my clients that my business mentor is for me. I coach professional women to overcome barriers and to embrace the next chapter of life. I feel good knowing that God is leading me now closer to His vision for my life and that these actions will help me to remain relevant in my sixties. As I've shared my faith throughout this book, I realize that there are women who don't believe that God can speak to them. I'm a witness that He can and will. His grace is beyond measure. Being able to hear the voice of God isn't dramatic like a full orchestra playing in the background. God will use people, your environment, and His still, small voice to speak to you. You may not believe in God. My intent isn't to sound preachy or to make you feel like you have to believe the same way I do. I feel the privilege to share with you the things that motivate me, cause me to be afraid, and how my faith in God brings me through my difficult times. He is always with me. These truths that I have shared will help you make changes in your life, motivate you, and help you accomplish your life's goals. I hope that the words have jumped off the pages and into your spirit with the tips that have resonated with you. I pray that you'll experience growth. I want you to win and make your mark in the world, no matter your age. Now you have somewhere to start and the tools necessary to make an impact.

The last thing up to this point that God has done for me was to download into my spirit the idea for this book. He provided me with every thought and teachable moment with the intent of the book being a gift to you. I'm thrilled that God continues to use and trust me to speak to the hearts and minds of women like you. I vow to remain connected and declare that I shall be healthy, successful, more than a conqueror, and relevant. I refuse to hide and I choose to tell women who I am, what I do, and how I can help them. I shall remain relevant, and therefore I'm no longer anxious about turning sixty! Thank you for sticking around to get tips to help you live your life out loud.

BE Brave-ER

What healthy plans have you adopted in your daily life and how have they impacted your overall health?

It is recommended that the average adult received 150 minutes of exercise per week. What is your plan for achieving this goal?

What exercises get you pump up and can become a daily routine?

If you've worked with a therapist, what are some of the benefits you received?

What activities can do to reduce your stressors?

What will you next brave and bold move look like?

During the pandemic was there a turning point where you experience a mind shift?

What growth opportunities have you started while on this journey and how have you applied them?

What is the one thing that God has place in your heart to do?

Chapter 7

Be-Brave-ER and Reach New Heights!

I love butterflies. Their beautiful and brightly-colored wings carry them to new heights. I'm captivated by their presence. While in their presence, I'm stretched and feel that much-needed push to take action in my life by creating new beginnings.

Much like humans, butterflies go through many changes. They experience a metamorphosis that consists of four stages before reaching their full development. Butterflies don't kick and scream when told that change is coming. They have no choice but to go with the flow. We hate change, but change is necessary. It provides us with an opportunity to become different while becoming brave-ER. Right now, you may resist change in your life. Your body language is evident in your resistance. Your body becomes tense at the mention of the word. You might have your guard up, purposely camouflaging your gifts, and you may find that your confidence is fleeting. It's okay to not feel okay, but it's not okay to stay in this place. We go through a metamorphosis of sorts like the butterfly. Change occurs in six stages: pre-contemplation, contemplation, preparation, action, maintenance, and termination. The stage we have focused on throughout this book is our ability to take action. Taking action is what makes us resilient. Embrace change to reach new heights. You got this!

What we resist is more than likely to haunt us and come back and bite us in the butt. Wouldn't it be fulfilling to allow your inner butterfly to see the light of day? You can achieve this by pledging yourself to commit to completing the goals you started. The bogeyman wants you to remain in a pre-contemplation state. God reminds us that if we resist the bogeyman he will flee. Be patient with yourself and work on one goal at a time. Declare that you will experience a breakthrough. The abundant life is at your fingertips as you embrace your metamorphosis. You will reap rewards such as experiencing a transformation, a renewed sense of confidence, and being immersed in a greater sense of hope. I can't think of any woman who wouldn't want to reap these benefits. You got this!

The secret to staying on a positive trajectory is to re-commit to being a presence in your life. Commit today. Repeat after me, "I (fill in your name), proclaim that today is the day that I will begin to live my best life." Imagine yourself changing and becoming the woman you want to be. We have to do our part to manifest what we want. Call it into existence. Write down your new commitments in a meaningful place and review them regularly. These steps are necessary to conquer the bogeyman. Tame him once and for all. Remember that you are in control. Utilize the following tools to help you.

First: Believe in yourself. The world is waiting to embrace your gifts that you are manifesting. If you haven't discovered what they are, think about tangible things that represent you. Be brave-ER by introducing them to future customers. You might have to dig deeper, but it's worth it. Key tip: Be brave-ER by being intentional as you begin to implement your goals.

> *Be brave-ER by being intentional as you begin to implement your goals.*

Second: Ask yourself how to set healthy boundaries for yourself. The Webster dictionary defines boundaries as, "something that indicates or fixes a limit or extent." There is nothing wrong with setting healthy boundaries around your personal space, ideas, needs, and with your family. When you don't set healthy boundaries, you are ultimately tethering yourself to other peoples' agendas and needs. The consequence of living life this way is that you'll never get on track or have an opportunity to accomplish the goals you value the most. It's exhausting to always have to cater to the whims of your husband, kids, and the other important people in your life. Key tip: Let go of the need to be a "people pleaser". Set healthy boundaries even if it means having to turn on a neon sign that warns: "BENITA'S NEEDS are being FULFILLED FIRST. Get in line to have yours fulfilled."

Don't be afraid to communicate your needs. Your family can't read your mind, so you have to use your words. Third, remember that love is a catalyst to push you forward as you take care of yourself and others. You've heard that saying, "You can help anyone until you help yourself." Loving yourself and others can be complicated, but it doesn't have to be that way.

Key Tip: Consider what God says about love in the Bible; it will make it easier for you to love others through times of displeasure with them. 1 Corinthians 13:4-5: "Love is patient, love is kind. It does not envy, it does not boast, it is not proud. It does not dishonor others, it is not self-seeking, it is not easily angered, it keeps no record of wrongs."

Love yourself enough to know that you are important and the world needs to experience more of you.

Fourth: Forgive yourself and others. Forgiveness is the most important step in the attainment of freedom. Forgiveness can set you free. Carrying the weight of unforgiveness is like carrying around a huge bowling ball. Anyone who has ever gone bowling knows that bowling balls are heavy. Throw the bowling ball down the lane, not allowing it to fall into the gutter. Let your grievances go and learn to forgive others instead. God can help you remove grievances from your heart and replace them with love and forgiveness if you ask Him.

Key tip: Forgiveness is not only for those who hurt you, but it's for *your* healing. God has equipped you with the capacity to forgive. Relax and carry-on. Forgive today!

Continue to grow! Lean in by making sure that you leave no stone unturned. A great way of achieving this is to identify causes and areas of development that speak to your spirit that you can share with other women. Women leading women is beneficial to our growth and development. This is something that I have found to be true in my life. Our bond as women is strong when we don't allow the bogeyman to get in the way by making things messy. I've learned to reach out to other women who are in my circle of trust or whose online presence resonates with me. Some of the avenues of learning have come in the form of listening to their podcasts, reading their books, attending specialized seminars, and my favorite activity by far — attending women's events.

I am always intrigued by what I'm able to glean from them and how comfortable I am while in their presence. Doing these things is a great way to get your feet wet and a great way to get comfortable in large group settings with other women. It could be the spark you need, and just like it was for me, a way to get off the sidelines. I believe that when women take actions like these, we do ourselves a service and an opportunity to collaborate. As women, we have shared experiences because of our DNA. Some of our uncomfortableness and non-trust of other women is based on fear and past experiences.

We still hold on to the fight we had with our friend, Lisa, who stabbed us in the back years ago. We're still sulking and waiting for an apology we will never get. This type of thinking is what keeps us stuck in the past. We end up missing opportunities meant for our growth. Women can be petty, but it's time to turn away from our comfortableness and stubbornness. Turn the page so that you can reach new heights.

Be bold and be brave-ER as you begin to establish new connections with women. If 2020 didn't teach us anything else, it taught us that time waits for no one and if we're willing to sit quietly and search our hearts for our purpose, we will find it.

What's your next move? Are you ready to conquer the bogeyman? He has taken up too much space in your head and too much time from your growth. It's time to take your power back in 2021 so that you will be equipped to be brave-ER.

Earlier we talked about the power of journaling. I will go as far as saying that I believe that journaling is step #1 to being brave-ER. It's the outlet that gives you permission to speak your truth on paper and reflect on your thoughts. For journaling to be effective, you have to do it daily until it becomes a habit. Journaling also provides you with a way to check in with yourself if you are not seeing a professional for therapy. Checking in with yourself is a great way to establish some accountability. As we discussed earlier, the best benefit of all is to tame the bogeyman who wants nothing more than to stop you from living your best life.

There will be some days when you can't think of anything to write about in your journal. I suggest that you use the journal prompts from the various questions at the end of each chapter in this book. Remember, I shared many things with you, like my childhood, my fears, motherhood, marriage, my failures, and my successes. These are great things to journal and are not unique to my life or experiences.

> *The goal is to tap into your innermost thoughts and to find peace amidst the storm.*

When journaling about self-development and discovery, here are some additional tips: 1) Use a fresh page to journal every morning before you begin your day. Write down 10-15 goals that come to mind and repeat this goal for thirty days without looking at the previous day. This will help you to re-visit all of the goals at the end of the thirty days. You may find some clarity about what's important to you. 2) Write down three things that you are grateful for over a period of thirty days. These grateful things, skills, or people in your life may help you work on those relationships or things by putting up boundaries so that you can continue to enjoy them long into the future. Remember, the goal is to tap into your innermost thoughts and to find peace amidst the storm.

I'd like to share a couple of writing prompts that I enjoy. They have provided me the freedom needed to address my fears and feelings of being boxed in. I would like for you to try them. They will boost your confidence, and you will become brave-ER. Wouldn't it feel great to reap the benefits that journaling provides, such as reducing stress, achieving clarity, and having the ability to move around your world freely with purpose?

First Writing Prompt: This prompt helps to address the things that make you afraid. Use a fresh sheet in your journal and please be honest with yourself as you write them down. I am providing you an example of my 'Dear, Fear' letter. It is important to address your fears and to record them on paper. You may find it more freeing than a therapy session. Once you complete it, you will have a powerful letter that you've poured your darkest fears onto the pages. This exercise will help you release some stress, worry, and anxiety. Don't worry about grammar or making the letter look pretty. You'll make numerous edits before it's all said and done and you have created one that will help you face your fears and feel brave-ER.

Disclaimer: I'm not in any way saying that doing this exercise will keep your fears from haunting you. However, it can be utilized as a tool in your *oversized* Louis Vuitton satchel to help you as needed to fight fear when fear shows up.

Second Writing Prompt: This prompt helps to address the feeling of others having control over you. It's a letter to the principal. Perhaps the principal in your life is a parent or another authority figure who's always riding your back and getting on your last nerve. We associate this person with the person who restricts us from our feelings, doing what we would like to do and being a jerk. It's the bogeyman in real life. I encourage you to let the "principal" know on pages of your journal that you're serious about getting your life and time back. Put him or her on notice by letting them know that from this day forward you're taking back your power. This writing prompt is my favorite of the two. By doing this exercise, I was able to see all the things or people that were limiting my progress by making me feel that I wasn't pretty enough, good enough, or brave enough. It also addressed the lie that the bogeyman told me that I didn't have what it takes to succeed. I believe wholeheartedly that women are the fiercest and most powerful forces on the planet. We can do anything that we put our minds to.

Always remember that you matter and that you get permission to be who you are, and you also get permission to have what you need to live your best life. Be proactive. I've enjoyed taking you on this journey of self-discovery that will lead you to be brave-ER. Go ahead! Be brave-ER — you deserve it.

BE Brave-ER

What journaling prompts have you used to bring you through difficult periods in your life?

How has the principal of your past mocked you and how will you take back your peace in the future?

What fears are you ready to conquer?

Are you ready to become the change agent of your life?

How can you can effectively communicate your boundaries to others?

What are some ways you can positivity embrace change?

The world is ready to see your bright colors how will you meet the moment?

_____

_____

Is giving yourself permission to live an abundant life is worth it?

_____

_____

_____

What life lessons you have gleaned from this journey?

_____

_____

What specific ways have you been transformed?

_____

_____

What positive affirmation are you willing to adopt and repeat daily?

_____

_____

_____

Will you take action today?

_____

_____

_____

BE
Brave-ER

Congratulations! You Made it to The End of The Book.
Go Ahead; Toot Your Horn!
Watch Out, World! Another Brave Soul is Being
Released to Live Life Out Loud!

Dear, Fear

Dear, Fear,

I'm Putting you on Notice! You no longer have permission to control my life. I have allowed you to manipulate me for far too long. You keep me at arms length from my dreams and desires that you know will ultimately propel me to greatness. On some level, you've convinced me to sit still and grumble about how I've allowed you to place things important to me on hold just to appease you. I've hidden under the guise that my purpose wasn't good enough and that I don't have what it takes to serve others. You've been successful at making me believe that and that I will never become a successful entrepreneur. You said that my God-given abilities are merely hobbies unworthy of providing me with income streams. Your roadblocks have distracted me far too long. You've sat on my shoulders for years, speaking into my spirit and spouting lies with the intention of stopping me. Congratulations! It worked and you have succeeded! My triggers with food were on high alert, causing me to eat more than I should have and I gained weight that led to my unhappiness. I've stood in front of the mirror in my underwear, ashamed of the person looking back at me. I've listened to your insults as you laughed at me and told me to hide my overweight body from the world. My gifts are strong, yet you helped me place them in the background as you tried every trick imaginable. But guess what? Your plot, FEAR, is no longer working. I've gotten out of my own way to help women who struggle just like me, and they are beginning to see the better parts of themselves too. Get this; your busted! I now control me. I've taking back my life and I vow to use my God-given gifts no matter what it takes. God makes no mistakes, and His arms are wrapped tightly around me. With God, I can't fail. Fear, you'd been replaced with Faith. Bye-bye, Fear. Hello, world; here I come!

No Longer Yours, Benita

Permission from the Principal's Office

Dear, Benita,

I am the principal and have granted you these permissions:

- ✔ You have permission to lose weight and to be healthy.

- ✔ You have permission to be honest.

- ✔ You have permission to say, "No," to others.

- ✔ You have permission to celebrate your wins in ways of your choosing.

- ✔ You have permission to wear a little black dress with sexy heels.

- ✔ You have permission to live your life out loud.

- ✔ You have permission to go on vacations anywhere in the world.

- ✔ You have permission to launch a successful coaching business.

- ✔ You have permission to be an awesome grandmother.

- ✔ You have permission to love your husband and to allow him to love you.

- ✔ You have permission to have wealth and to enjoy it.

- ✔ You have permission to feel special.

- ✔ You have permission to coach others to be the best version of themselves.

- ✔ You have permission to want the best for your adult children.

- ✔ You have permission to be okay with others' envy.

- ✔ You have permission to reap the rewards of your creativity.

- ✔ You have permission to grow your circle of influence.

- ✔ You have permission to not care if others don't like you.

- ✔ You have permission to be healthy emotionally and spiritually.

- ✔ You have permission to ask God for a favor and know you will get it.

- ✔ You have permission to remind yourself that you belong to God.

- ✔ You have permission to pray for your kids, husband, and yourself daily.

About The Author

Benita Tyler, the author of *Addicted to Dysfunction: Release to Live Life Out Loud, Put Up or Get Shut Down, Wayward Sisters,* and *Wayward Sisters (2),* among other works, lives in Kokomo, Indiana, with her husband, Cedric Tyler. She is a life coach, ghostwriter, physical trainer, mother, and doting grandmother. Her work across multiple disciplines broadly addresses the narrative of women's adversities. Her motivational spirit and example serve to edify the lives of everyone she touches. Benita is resilient and has survived life's hard knocks. In her professional life, she is a lifelong learner who has an MBA in Business Administration, Bachelors of Science Degree in Management, Associates of Science Degree in Business, and a Graduate Certificate in Human Resources. She would like to be a prolific blessing and inspiration to those through her writings.

Also by
BENITA TYLER

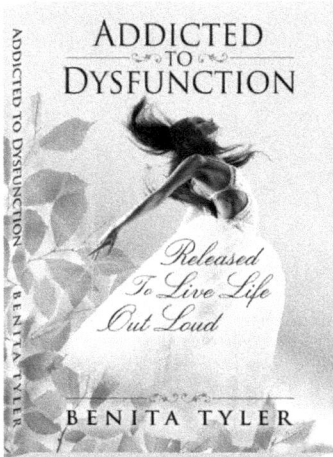

Addicted to Dysfunction: Released to Live Life Out Loud
is the first book written that allows the reader to take an inconspicuous analysis of their own life's dysfunction through an honest account of the writer's sufferings and the lessons learned from them. This book is divided into five main character sections. The first section tackles disappointment. The second section stresses the importance of relational choices. The third section examines forgiveness. The forth section awakens our awareness. The fifth section challenges our acceptance of others. Collectively, these lessons will challenge you to let go and let God — releasing the reader to live life out loud.

Hardcover ISBN 978-0-9856964-0-5 • Softcover ISBN 978-0-9856964-1-2
eBook ISBN 978-0-9856964-2-9

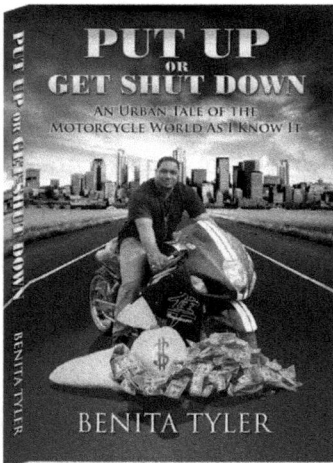

Put Up Or Get Shut Down is a bold and sassy "up in your face" excursion into the urban motorcycle world as the writer knows it. Salty Dog is a narcissistic brother with an ego big enough to match the horsepower of his chrome 1300 Suzuki Hayabusa. Throughout this epic journey, you'll learn about those scandalous women who lurk around the urban motorcycle community looking for a chance to get a "ride" in one form or another from the motorcycle brothers. This ride will be entertaining, and you'll either have to put up or get shut down for trying to flee from this urban tale.

Softcover ISBN 978-0-9856964-3-6 • eBook ISBN 978-0-9856964-4-3

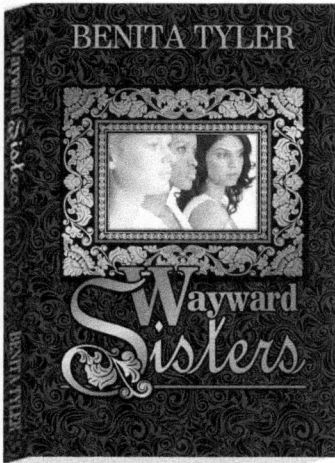

Wayward Sisters

Imagine a beautiful place where secrets are told and reconciliation is at your fingertips. Boyfriend drama, parental disputes, and betrayal are the backdrop to the demise of a twenty year friendship. Keisha, Megan, and Natalia experience all this and more. Will the Wayward Sisters seek the path that God desires for them before it's too late? Come along on this captivating journey as good and bad choices are made that will leave you at the edge of your seat thirsting for more.

Softcover ISBN 978-0-9856964-5-0

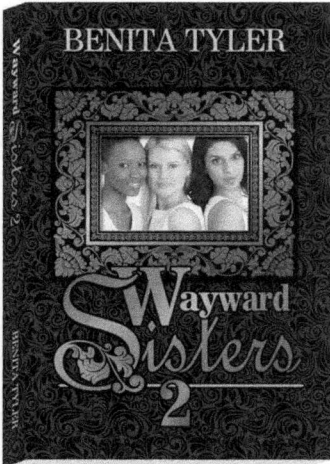

Wayward Sisters 2

Keisha, Megan, and Natalia are back at it again on a quest to experience God's best through personal growth and the strength of their beautiful sisterhood. Jada, David, and Terrance, siblings of Keisha, join them on this captivating journey to ensure the historical family church, Victory Baptist Church, where they are employed, brings them growth and a stronger sense of faith. Will the Wayward Sisters finally find love, or will their relationships be tested to the point of no return? You'll have to buckle in to see how their place of reckoning helps them escape self-deprivation and how it is replaced with self-love.

Softcover ISBN 978-0-9856964-8-1

Beloved Daffodil's Inspirations
700 E. Firmin Street, Suite 188 Kokomo, IN 46902
www.BelovedDaffodilsInspirations.com

www.ingramcontent.com/pod-product-compliance
Lightning Source LLC
Chambersburg PA
CBHW071607040426
42452CB00008B/1270